Frederick Douglass

Frederick Douglass
A NOBLE LIFE

David A. Adler

Holiday House ❧ New York

For Renée
again and forever

꙳

The publisher wishes to thank Professor William E. Cain,
of Wellesley College, for his comments on the manuscript.

Library of Congress Cataloging-in-Publication Data
Adler, David A.
Frederick Douglass : a noble life / by David A. Adler. — 1st ed.
p. cm.
Includes bibliographical references.
ISBN 978-0-8234-2056-8 (hardcover)
1. Douglass, Frederick, 1818-1895—Juvenile literature. 2. Abolitionists—United States—
Biography—Juvenile literature. 3. African American abolitionists—Biography—Juvenile
literature. 4. Antislavery movements—United States—Juvenile literature. I. Title.
E449.D75A34 2010
973.7'114092—dc22
[B]
2009029970

CONTENTS

PREFACE

Frederick Douglass was born a slave, who with his strength of character and great intelligence transformed himself into one of America's foremost citizens. He was a lecturer, author, editor, bank president, ambassador, reformer, human rights advocate and friend and advisor of President Lincoln. At his death it was said, "No man started so low and climbed so high as he."

Here is a detailed picture of slavery in America and Douglass' escape, a thrilling story of courage and great adventure. Once free, he fought for the freedom of others and his abolition activities won him the title, "father of the protest movement." He was a friend of Susan B. Anthony and one of the early supporters of women's rights. He joined the protests of the tragic lynchings that began near the end of the nineteenth century. This story follows Douglass across the American continent, to Europe, Egypt, and Greece, and because he wrote three autobiographies, gave thousands of well-attended lectures, and edited an abolitionist journal, many of the words in this book are his.

Frederick Douglass at work

Chapter One ✳ ━━━━━━━━━━━━━━━━━━━━━━━━

"I SOBBED MYSELF TO SLEEP"

Harriet Beecher Stowe

"I hate him! And isn't he mine?
Can't I do what I like with him?"
. . . the spirit of evil came back with seven-fold vehemence,
and Legree, foaming with rage, smote his victim to the ground.

—From the novel *Uncle Tom's Cabin*, by Harriet Beecher Stowe, a book that
exposed nineteenth-century readers to the horrors of slavery,

Frederick douglass was born a slave, and as a teenager, he worked for
Edward Covey, an especially cruel master.

Covey provided little for his slaves to eat and not enough time for sleep.
The work was constant, even in the worst weather. "Work, work, work,"
Douglass later remembered, was "the order of the day." Covey would send the
sixteen-year-old Douglass out, and then hide in ditches or behind trees and
fence posts. When Douglass stopped to rest, even for just a moment, Covey
snuck up and whipped, kicked, and clubbed him.

Douglass was "completely wrecked, changed, and bewildered," he later wrote,
"goaded almost to madness." He was tempted to take his own life. Then, one very
hot day in August 1834, he reached his breaking point. Covey hit him, and he hit
back. Douglass grabbed Covey by his throat and threw him to the ground.

"Are you going to resist, you scoundrel?" Covey asked.

Douglass answered a polite "yes sir."

Every blow to Douglass was returned. Again and again, the young slave threw his tormentor to the ground.

Covey called to his cousin, who joined the fight. But Douglass would not be stopped. Soon the cousin was bent over in pain. Covey called to two other slaves, but they both refused to help.

After two hours, Covey got up, bloodied, and declared, "I would not have whipped you half so much as I have had you not resisted."

But Douglass later wrote, "The fact was, he had not whipped me at all."

Douglass could have been beaten in public for his defiance, as a warning to other slaves. He could have been hanged. But Covey was ashamed to speak of the incident, to let others know he had been mastered by a young slave. And he never hit Douglass again.

The fight was a turning point for Douglass. It relit the fire for freedom that burned within him. "I was *nothing* before," Douglass later wrote. "I WAS A MAN NOW."

🌸

FREDERICK DOUGLASS was born in Tuckahoe, Maryland, on the tobacco, corn, and wheat farm of Captain Aaron Anthony, the manager of the estates of Colonel Edward Lloyd. Douglass's mother, Harriet Bailey, was an African American slave. He never knew who his father was, though it was said he was a white man, and rumored to be Aaron Anthony. Douglass also never knew his birth date. In fact, he didn't even know the year. He thought he was born in February 1817, but a slave journal later proved it had been 1818.

Harriet Bailey named her son Frederick Augustus Washington Bailey, a grand name for a child she would hardly know. Later, when he escaped from slavery, he changed his name to Frederick Douglass in order to fool anyone who might come looking for him.

Soon after Douglass was born, he was taken from his mother. This was a common practice for slave owners. Without a child to care for, a slave could get back to work as a field hand. Also, by separating slave mothers from their children, family attachments were weakened. This made it easier to sell young slaves off and send them away. Sadly, Douglass remembered seeing his mother only four or five times and always at night, after her work was done. "She would lie down with me," he later wrote, "and get me to sleep, but long before I waked she was gone."

Douglass spent his early years with his grandparents, Isaac and Betsey Bailey, who lived in a one-room windowless cabin built of wood, straw, and clay, in woods owned by Captain Anthony. Isaac Bailey was a free man, a woodcutter. Betsey Bailey made fishnets, was a nurse, and was known for the sweet potatoes she grew. It was said she brought good luck to the fields she worked in, and that anything she planted was sure to flourish.

Betsey Bailey was a slave, but she "enjoyed the high privilege," Douglass later wrote, "of living in a cabin, separate from the quarter, with no other burden than her own support, and the necessary care of the little children." She had five daughters and a son, about Douglass's age, who were all slaves.

Douglass's years in his grandparents' home were happy. "My grandmother! My grandmother!" Douglass later wrote. "The little hut and the joyous circle under her care, but especially *she*, who made us sorry when she left us but for an hour, and glad on her return."

In 1855, Douglass, looking back at his early childhood, mused at the odd irony of the carefree upbringing of a slave boy compared with that of privileged white boys. The young slave, he wrote, "is never chided for handling his little knife and

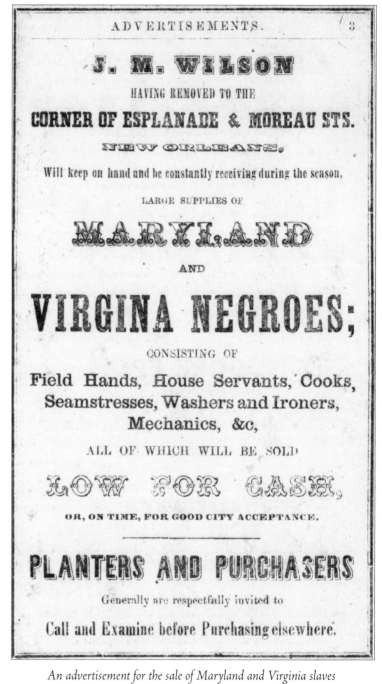

An advertisement for the sale of Maryland and Virginia slaves

fork improperly or awkwardly, for he uses none. He is never reprimanded for soiling the tablecloth for he takes his meals on the clay floor. He never has the misfortune in his games or sports of soiling or tearing his clothes, for he has almost none to soil or tear. He is never expected to act like a nice little gentleman for he is only a rude little slave. . . . He literally runs wild."

But whatever joy and whatever freedoms he felt as a young slave were short-lived.

In 1824, on a beautiful August morning, his grandmother took him for a twelve-mile walk. "The journey would have proved too severe for me," Douglass later wrote, "but that my dear old grandmother (blessings on her memory) afforded occasional relief by 'toteing' me on her shoulder."

By afternoon, six-year-old Frederick Douglass saw some "great houses" in the distance and many men and women working in the fields. "Grandmamma looked sad. She was soon to lose another object of affection, as she had lost many before. I knew she was unhappy, and the shadow fell from her brow on me, though I knew not the cause."

Soon Douglass came to Colonel Lloyd's house. It was surrounded by children he described as "of many colors; black, brown, copper colored, and nearly white." His grandmother patted him on his head, told him to be a good boy, and encouraged him to go and play. "They are kin to you," she said, and pointed to two girls and a boy. They were his sisters and brother: Sarah, Eliza, and Perry. But Douglass didn't know them. "Slavery," he later wrote, "had made us strangers."

Douglass followed the children into a big house. He stood and watched the others play until one of them said, "Fed, Fed, Grandmamma gone!"

Betsey Bailey had left her grandson in the house of strangers.

Young Frederick Douglass felt betrayed. Years later, he wrote that he didn't know what happened next, "but I suppose I sobbed myself to sleep."

Chapter Two

"MANY CHILDREN, BUT NO FAMILY"

The very earliest thing that I remember was the selling of my mother.
I must have been about two years old then. . . .
My father was sold before I was born, and I know nothing of him.
I had one brother, three or four years older than myself, and eight sisters.
Some of my sisters were early sold away,
and I do not know whether they are alive or not.

—Thomas Rutling, a former slave, 1872

On that beautiful August day in 1824, Betsey Bailey left six-year-old Frederick Douglass at Colonel Lloyd's "great house." Young Douglass didn't know the harsh realities of slavery. What he saw was a large white home with a wide front porch. He later wrote that it "was a treat to my young and gradually opening mind to behold this elaborate exhibition of wealth, power, and beauty." The house was the grandest building he had ever seen.

A plantation "great house,"
Tuckahoe, Maryland

Visitors entered the property through a high gate and walked or rode on a quarter-mile-long circular lane covered with white pebbles, past a front lawn of lush grass with patches of flowers and ornamental trees that sheltered a flock of red-winged blackbirds, and beyond the lane were rabbits and deer. The nearby creeks had fish, crabs, clams, and oysters. In the distance, boats made their way to and from Baltimore.

The great house was surrounded by smaller buildings—summer houses; greenhouses; separate hen, turkey, and pigeon huts; a cooking house; a wash house; and a dairy. All were well kept. Along the walks were trellises covered with flowering vines, and stately ornamental trees. About a mile off was a windmill that young Douglass loved to watch as its large white sails slowly spun.

Years later, Douglass wrote that immense wealth "filled the Great House with all that can please the eye, or tempt the taste." The Lloyds, who lived there, dressed in "purple and fine linen." They slept on feather beds and down-filled pillows. And the meals! "The table groans under the heavy and blood-bought luxuries gathered with pains-taking care, at home and abroad." Almost sixty years later, Douglass remembered the "unending rounds of feasting" on chicken, turkeys, ducks, geese, beef, and veal, as well as "the teeming riches of the Chesapeake Bay . . . trout, oyster, crabs, and terrapin" and "fragrant cheese, golden butter, and delicious cream."

For Douglass, "the greatest attraction of the place" was the lavish, manicured garden. People came from "far and near," he wrote, "from Baltimore, Easton, and Annapolis," to see it. The garden "abounded in fruits of almost every description, from the hardy apple of the north to the delicate orange of the south." Those fruits were a great temptation to the underfed slaves. Just about every day during the summer, a slave was whipped for eating them. That all stopped when the fence surrounding the garden was coated with tar. If a slave was caught stained with it, he or she was whipped. "This plan worked well," Douglass wrote. "The slaves became as fearful of tar as of the lash."

Young Frederick Douglass was considered the "property" of Aaron Anthony, a former seagoing ship's captain who now owned three farms and had some thirty slaves. But Anthony's greatest responsibilities were managing the more than twenty farms and one thousand slaves belonging to one of the richest, most powerful men in America, Colonel Edward Lloyd. Lloyd had been a United States congressman and the governor of Maryland. When Douglass was taken to his plantation, Lloyd was a United States senator.

There was a less glorious side to Lloyd's estate: the slave dwellings.

Slaves were crowded into dilapidated shacks. Men and women, boys and girls—all slept together on the clay floor, which was often wet and cold. The adults had coarse blankets. The children had none, and tried to find warm corners or places near the chimney so that they could stick their feet in the ashes and keep warm as they slept.

Slave children on the Lloyd farms were given very little to wear. Douglass had only a rough sackcloth shirt that barely reached his knees. He wore it day and night and got to change it just once a week. During winter, with so little to wear, he tried to keep warm by staying on the sunny side of the house by day and crawling into a bag of corn at night.

Meals for slaves were meager. The children were given cornmeal mush, which was poured into a large tray or trough. They were called to eat "like so many pigs," Douglass later wrote, "and like so many pigs would come, some

A slave cabin

Gone off with the Y.

with oyster shells, some with pieces of shingles, but none with spoons, and literally devour the mush." The strongest child got the best spot by the trough; the fastest eater got the most. Few left really satisfied.

Adult slaves on the Lloyd farm had a monthly food allowance of cornmeal, salt, and pickled pork or fish, but this was hardly enough. To supplement their diet, at night and on Sundays Lloyd's slaves fished for oysters.

Every morning, at daybreak, the overseer stood by the door to the slave cabin with a stick and an ox-hide whip that was as hard as wood. He blew a horn, and there was a rush. The slaves knew the last one out was sure to be beaten. "More slaves were whipped for oversleeping," Douglass wrote in 1855, "than for any other fault."

When the workday ended, slaves were expected to prepare and eat their meals, wash themselves, and clean and mend their clothes. If their tools needed sharpening or fixing, they did that, too. At night, they often fell to the floor exhausted and slept until morning.

Lloyd had too many slaves to know them all, and many did not know him. A chance meeting, retold by Douglass in 1845, gives the sad picture of slave life on the Lloyd plantation.

While riding along the road one day, Lloyd met a slave. "'Well, boy, who do you belong to?' 'To Colonel Lloyd,' replied the slave. 'Well, does the colonel treat you well?' 'No, sir' was the ready reply. 'What! does he work you too hard?' 'Yes, sir.' 'Well, don't he give you enough to eat?' 'Yes, sir, he gives me enough, such as it is.'"

The slave didn't know he had met his master until a few weeks later, when he was handcuffed, locked in chains, taken from his family and friends, and sold to a Georgia trader. "*This* is the penalty," Douglass wrote, "of telling the simple truth, in answer to a series of plain questions."

Frederick Douglass was put in the care of Colonel Lloyd's cook, "Aunt Katy"—called "Aunt" because of her age and position. Douglass described her as "ambitious, ill-tempered, and cruel." She once chased her own son Phil with a large butcher knife, slashed him, and left a deep cut near his wrist. But mostly Aunt Katy didn't strike out at her charges—she starved them.

A slave kitchen

"Want of food was my chief trouble the first summer," Douglass later wrote. "I speak the simple truth when I say I have often been so pinched with hunger that I have fought with the dog 'Old Nep' for the smallest crumbs that fell from the kitchen table and have been glad when I won a single crumb in the combat. Many times have I followed with eager step the waiting girl when she went out to shake the table cloth to get the crumbs and small bones flung out for the cats."

He did not get along with Aunt Katy. He later remembered that his offenses were many, and one day she took to "her favorite mode of punishing me, namely, making me go without food all day—that is, from after breakfast."

Douglass doubted he could last much beyond sundown, when he was usually given a slice of corn bread. "Sundown came, but no bread." While she distributed thick slices of bread to the other children, Katy told him that she meant to starve the life out of him and she gave none to Douglass. With that, he went out behind the house and cried.

Later, he returned to the kitchen and sat by the fire, too hungry to sleep. He happened to look up and notice an ear of corn on a high shelf. He climbed up, took off a few kernels, and roasted them in the hot ashes. Then, just as he was about to eat his meager "meal," his mother came in.

Harriet Bailey had walked twelve miles to see her son. "The friendless and hungry boy," Douglass wrote in 1845, "found himself in the strong, protecting arms of a mother." Douglass told her he had not eaten since morning, that Aunt Katy meant to starve him. His mother took the kernels of corn from Frederick and gave him a ginger cake in the shape of a heart. Then she scolded Katy.

"That night I learned as I had never learned before that I was not only a child, but somebody's child. I was grander upon my mother's knee than a king upon his throne."

Douglass fell asleep. When he awoke, his mother was gone. He never saw her again. Harriet Bailey died when Frederick Douglass was about seven years old. "I was not allowed to be present during her illness, at her death, or burial," he wrote. "She was gone long before I knew anything about it." Later, he was told his mother could read, a real achievement for a slave who had never gone to school. He credited her with his love of words and thirst for knowledge.

"My poor mother," Douglass wrote mournfully in 1855, "like so many other slave-women, had many children, but no family!"

Chapter Three

"WHY AM I A SLAVE?"

[The old captain] was noted for severity to his servants.
It was said that he had killed a man named Reuben
and a woman named Rachel by excessive beating.
He had lately struck, with a heavy club, a poor old man
who used to tend him when a baby.
—JAMES FISHER, A SLAVE IN TENNESSEE AND LOUISIANA

SLAVES WERE NOT all treated the same, even those with the same master. Owners of large plantations often left field slaves to cruel white overseers, whose only concern was forcing as much work as they could out of their "human cattle." House slaves, such as cooks, maids, and nurses, were treated better. Some slaves had trades. They were carpenters, carriage makers, shoemakers, lumberjacks, blacksmiths, printers, and factory workers. They were of great value to their slaveholders, who could set up shops for them and profit from their work, or rent them out by the day. As a mark of respect, these skilled men were often called "Uncle" by the younger slaves. On the Lloyd plantation, "Uncle Tony" was the blacksmith, "Uncle Abel" was the shoemaker, and "Uncle Harry" was the carriage maker. "Uncle Isaac Copper" was the slaves' doctor and minister, and young Douglass was sent to him to learn religion.

Copper was disabled and got around on crutches. When Douglass first met him, he was seated on a large stool. Nearby were some hickory switches, long enough for him to reach any child in the room. He told the more than twenty children present to kneel, and then had them repeat after him as he recited the Lord's Prayer.

"Everybody, in the south, seemed to want the privilege of whipping somebody else," Douglass wrote when telling of his first meeting with Uncle Isaac Copper. "'Say everything I say;' and bang would come the switch on some poor boy's undevotional head. *What you looking at there*'—'*Stop that pushing*'—and down again would come the lash."

Douglass didn't learn to love God and religion from Isaac Copper. He later wrote, "There was even at that time something a little inconsistent and laughable in my mind in the blending of prayer and punishment."

Douglass didn't hate Copper, or even his master. "The slaveholder, as well as the slave," Douglass wrote in 1881, "was the victim of the slave system." He knew what it had done to Captain Aaron Anthony.

"Could the reader have seen Captain Anthony gently leading me by the hand, as he sometimes did, patting me on the head, speaking to me in soft caressing tones and calling me his little Indian boy"—a nickname given to Douglass because of his copper-like skin color, high cheekbones, and wide-set eyes—"he would have deemed him a kind-hearted old man." But after a few months on his farm, Douglass saw that his outwardly gentle master could "commit outrages deep, dark, and nameless."

Anthony was a troubled, unhappy man. When he walked alone, he muttered to himself, and sometimes when no one but the slave children were nearby, he waved his arms, shook his head, snapped his fingers, and shouted at what Douglass called "an army of invisible foes."

Douglass also saw the cruel side of Anthony.

One day, Douglass's cousin ran more than ten miles barefooted to Anthony for protection from Mr. Plummer, her drunken, abusive overseer, who had whipped and beaten her with a wooden club. Her face was covered with blood. Her neck and shoulders were scarred. But instead of helping her, Anthony said she had gotten what she deserved, that she had better go back to Plummer immediately or he, Anthony, would whip what was left of her.

Douglass saw Captain Anthony beat Esther, his aunt, whom he described as "tall, well formed, and made a fine appearance." Good looks, Douglass wrote, "is ever a curse to the slave-girl." Esther was romantically involved with Ned Roberts, a "fine looking" slave. Anthony disapproved of the relationship and told Esther she would be severely punished if he ever saw her with Roberts.

Later, Anthony saw them together. Douglass witnessed Esther's beating and described it in his autobiography.

It was early in the morning, when all was still, and before any of the family in the house or kitchen had risen. I was, in fact, awakened by the heart-rending shrieks and piteous cries of poor Esther. My sleeping-place was on the dirt floor of a little rough closet which opened into the kitchen, and through the cracks in its unplaned boards I could distinctly see and hear what was going on, without being seen. Esther's wrists were firmly tied, and the twisted rope was fastened to a strong iron staple in a heavy wooden beam above, near the fireplace. Here she stood on a bench, her arms tightly drawn above her head. Her back and shoulders were perfectly bare. Behind her stood old master, with cowhide in hand, pursuing his barbarous work with all manner of harsh, coarse, and tantalizing epithets. He was cruelly deliberate, and protracted the torture as one who was delighted with the agony of his victim. Again and again he drew the hateful scourge through his hand, adjusting it with a view of dealing the most pain-giving blow his strength and skill could inflict. Poor Esther had never before been severely whipped. Her shoulders were plump and tender. Each blow, vigorously laid on, brought screams from her as well as blood. "Have mercy! Oh, mercy!" she cried. "I won't do so no more." But her piercing cries seemed only to increase his fury.

When Anthony untied Esther, she could hardly stand. Young Douglass, who had watched it all, was "terrified, hushed, stunned, and bewildered."

It was one of many beatings Douglass witnessed. He saw Nelly, one of Colonel Lloyd's slaves, punished for "impudence," perhaps a wrong look or gesture; or maybe the overseer, Mr. Sevier, was simply in the mood to punish a slave. Sevier grabbed Nelly, but she fought back until both she and the overseer were bloodied. "Let my mammy go! Let my mammy go!" her children screamed. At last, the overseer overpowered Nelly and tied her to a tree. He cursed and whipped her without mercy. And she cursed him back.

Douglass admired the fight in Nelly. He felt it served her well. "He was whipped oftener who was whipped easiest," he wrote. "The slave who had the courage to stand up for himself against the overseer, although he might have many hard stripes at first, became while legally a slave virtually a freeman."

Of course, there was no guarantee that resisting an overseer would be without consequences. Bill Denby was a young, hardworking slave who had offended Austin Gore, an overseer on the Lloyd plantation. Gore began to beat Denby, who, after a few blows, broke free, ran to the creek, and stood in water up to his neck. Gore ordered Denby to come out to take his punishment. Denby refused. Gore took out a pistol and with one shot killed the man. Bill Denby fell, with only the rising pool of blood to mark his grave.

The horrors young Frederick Douglass saw led him to question the nature of slavery. "Why am I a slave?" he wondered. "Why are some people slaves and others masters?" He asked his playmates, and they told him it was God's work to make black people slaves and white people their masters. But Douglass knew there were black people who were free and whites who were not slaveholders. Color could not be the answer.

A master and his overseer

Despite the torturous treatment around him, he later wrote, "I have nothing cruel or shocking to relate of my personal experiences while I remained on Colonel Lloyd's plantation. An occasional cuff from Aunt Katy and a regular whipping from old master such as any heedless and mischievous boy might get from his father is all I can mention of this sort."

Douglass was still not old enough to be a field slave, so he was left to bring the cows in at nightfall, keep the front yard clean, and do errands for Captain Anthony's daughter, Lucretia, who was married to Thomas Auld.

Miss Lucretia, as the children called her, was kind to Douglass. Once, he was hit on the forehead with a piece of metal by another boy. Aunt Katy told him it surely served him right, but Miss Lucretia cleaned and bandaged the wound. Other times, when Douglass was especially hungry, he would sing by her window and she would give him a buttered slice of bread.

It was Miss Lucretia who told Douglass the good news that the "old master" was sending him to Baltimore to serve Mr. Hugh Auld, the brother of her husband.

Douglass was ecstatic. He knew that whatever privations Baltimore might have in store for him, he had suffered them before. And he had heard exciting things about the city from his cousin Tom, who had been there. Tom told him the plantation's great house "was nothing to Baltimore." Tom reported on the *Baltimore in the 1800s*

displays in store windows, the uniformed soldiers, and the fireworks he had seen. He had even seen a steamboat.

Douglass had three days to prepare for the move, and he spent much of the time in the creek washing off plantation dirt. Miss Lucretia had promised him a pair of pants, his first, if he was properly cleaned.

When he sailed off, Douglass looked back at Colonel Lloyd's plantation, hoping it would be his last view of it or any place like it. Then he looked at the water ahead. The great world beyond the plantation was opening to eight-year-old Frederick Douglass, and he was eager to see it.

The trip took one day. The ship docked, and Douglass helped take the flock of sheep that was on board to market. Then he was brought to his new home, where he met his new mistress and master, Sophia and Hugh Auld, and their two-year-old son, Thomas.

Douglass was immediately taken with Miss Sophia, who showed real interest in him. He sensed kindness in her and was happy in his new home. "I had been treated as a *pig* on the plantation," he later wrote. "I was being treated as a *child* now."

He had decent meals and slept on a good straw bed, under real blankets. He had proper, clean clothes. In return, he ran errands and kept Thomas safe in the busy Baltimore streets.

Douglass noticed a marked difference in the treatment of city slaves. He saw that they were much better fed, better clothed, and happier than those on the Lloyd plantation. The ever-reflective Douglass felt it was the close living quarters of city life that kept slaveholders more civil. No one, he thought, wanted to be known by his neighbors as a cruel master.

Of course, city life was no guarantee of better treatment. The Hamiltons, who lived directly across from the Aulds, had two female house slaves, Henrietta and Mary—one twenty-two years old; the other, fourteen. Mrs. Hamilton, an outwardly charming woman, sat in a rocking chair singing sweet hymns . . . with a heavy leather whip at her side. "I speak within the truth," Douglass wrote, "when I say, that those girls seldom passed that chair during the day, without a blow from that cowskin, either upon their bare arms or upon their shoulders. As they passed her she would draw her cowskin and give them a blow saying 'move faster, you black jip!' and again, 'take that, you black jip!' continuing 'if you don't move faster I will give you more.'" In addition to the whippings, they were half-starved. Douglass wrote, "They seldom knew what it was to eat a full meal. I have seen Mary contending with the pigs for the offal thrown into the street."

In November 1826, after Douglass had been in Baltimore a year and a half, Captain Anthony died. His children had to divide his belongings, including his many slaves, so in March 1827, nine-year-old Frederick Douglass was sent back to the Lloyd plantation.

Douglass, Sophia, Hugh, and Thomas Auld all cried, knowing they might never be together again. For Douglass, there was the added humiliation that he would be reckoned among the property of his former master. "Men and women, young and old, married and single, were ranked with horses, sheep, and swine," he wrote—judged in dollar terms. "Silvery-headed age and sprightly youth, maids and matrons, had to undergo the same indelicate inspection. At this moment, I saw more clearly than ever the brutalizing effects of slavery upon both slave and slaveholder."

After each slave, each animal, each acre of land was given a value, the property would be divided. Parents and children, husbands and wives, would surely be separated. With the division would come a new master, and Douglass feared his would be Captain Anthony's cruel son Andrew, who was a drunk—and, what was even more frightening, a terrible money manager. Douglass and others knew Andrew could quickly lose his inheritance and need to sell his slaves. This was a prospect, Douglass wrote, that he "attended with fear

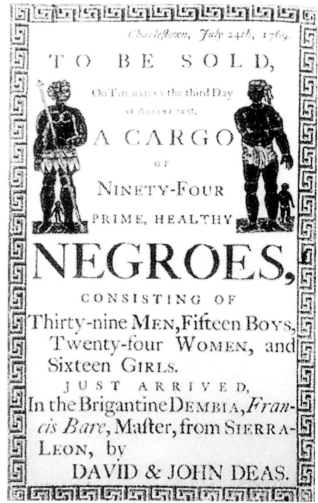

A 1769 poster advertising a slave sale

and dread," because then there would be little hope of ever again seeing his family and friends.

Just a few days before Captain Anthony's property was divided, Douglass saw Master Andrew grab his brother, Perry, by the throat, throw him to the ground, and step on his head until his nose and ears gushed blood. Andrew warned Douglass that soon he'd get the same treatment. "I could see," Douglass wrote later, "that he really thirsted to get hold of me."

But when the slaves were divided, Douglass became part of Thomas Auld's share, and he was returned to the Aulds of Baltimore. Douglass's entire time away had been just one month.

A slave auction in Richmond, Virginia, from an engraving published in an 1856 issue of
The Illustrated London News

Chapter Four

"THE TURNING POINT"

All these creatures get used to it;
it's the only way they can be kept in order.
　　—MARIE ST. CLAIRE IN *Uncle Tom's Cabin*,
　　CONCERNING THE WHIPPING OF A SLAVE

DOUGLASS SPENT the next five years in Baltimore. He helped around the house, watched over Thomas, and worked at Hugh Auld's shipyard.

When Hugh Auld was out, his wife often read the Bible. Douglass watched her and asked if she would teach him to read, so Miss Sophia taught him the alphabet and to read words of three and four letters. She was so proud of her student that she told her husband what she had done.

Hugh Auld was appalled. He told his wife that teaching a slave to read was against the law, that it could only lead to mischief. He felt a slave "should know nothing but to obey his master—to do as he is told to do." He warned that once Douglass could read there would be "no keeping him," that it would make him dissatisfied and unhappy.

Auld's strong reprimand was a revelation to Douglass. It taught him the power of the written word, that it was his path to freedom. If ignorance kept him in slavery, then knowledge would set him free.

Miss Sophia stopped the lessons, but Douglass didn't stop learning. Whenever he left the house on an errand, he carried along Thomas's old Webster's spelling book. He sometimes found stray pages from well-used Bibles in the streets. He washed the pages and dried them, and whenever he could, he read them. He pressed his young white playmates for reading lessons.

After Douglass learned to read, he taught himself to write. He copied letters from the spelling book. With chalk, he practiced writing on the sidewalk. When he was alone at home, he wrote in Thomas's old school workbooks.

The words Douglass copied from the Bible made a great impression on him. "I finally found that change of heart which comes by 'casting all one's care' upon God," he later wrote. "After this I saw the world in a new light."

While running errands, he met Lawson, a pious old black carriage driver who prayed three times a day and recited Bible passages as he walked in the street. Douglass became attached to him. They spent much of their free time together, and on Sundays, Douglass joined Lawson at prayer meetings.

Douglass was the better reader, so he taught his friend the *letter* while Lawson taught him the *spirit* of the words. The old man saw greatness in Douglass. He told him that God had work for him to do, that he must prepare himself for it. He convinced Douglass that with faith, all things are possible.

Perhaps Hugh Auld was right about the dangers of teaching a slave to read. Douglass became dissatisfied with his lot and later wrote that he "often wished myself a beast or a bird—anything, rather than a slave. I was wretched and gloomy beyond my ability to describe. I was too thoughtful to be happy."

He became obsessed with thoughts of liberty. "I saw nothing without seeing it," he later wrote, "and I heard nothing without hearing it. I do not exaggerate when I say that it looked from every star, smiled in every calm, breathed in every wind, and moved in every storm."

Liberty would one day come to Frederick Douglass, but not before he returned to Tuckahoe. He was sent back because of a misunderstanding between the brothers Thomas and Hugh Auld.

Henny, one of Thomas's slaves at Tuckahoe, had accidentally burnt her hands. After that, as a worker, "she was considered hardly worth the having—

of little more value than a horse with a broken leg," Douglass wrote. "This unprofitable piece of human property, ill-shapen and disfigured, Captain Auld sent off to Baltimore." Auld expected his brother, Hugh, to welcome her services.

Hugh soon decided that he had no use for Henny, and so he sent her back. This angered Thomas, who declared, "If he cannot keep *Hen* he shall not have *Fred.*"

It was 1833, seven years since Douglass's arrival in Baltimore. The Aulds, who had been so warm and welcoming to Douglass at first, had changed. Hugh Auld had a drinking problem. Sophia Auld no longer acted as kindly toward Douglass. Young Thomas was older and now thought of Douglass as his servant, not his playmate. Still, Douglass didn't want to leave them. He had many friends nearby, including a few young slaves whom he had taught to read. Also, he knew his best chances of escaping slavery were in a large city such as Baltimore.

When he returned to Thomas Auld, Douglass learned that Lucretia was gone. She had died, and Auld had remarried. His second wife, Rowena Hambleton Auld, was the daughter of a wealthy farmer, and Douglass saw them as a well-matched pair: He was stingy, and she was mean.

At Tuckahoe, Douglass was hungry again. Thomas Auld's slaves had to either beg for food or steal it to survive. "I frankly confess," Douglass later wrote, "that while I hate everything like stealing, *as such,* I nevertheless did not hesitate to take food, when I was hungry, wherever I could find it."

Douglass decided that since his body and his labor were the "property" of Thomas Auld and that the food he took was needed to enable him to serve Auld, it really wasn't stealing. He was simply "taking his meat out of one tub and putting it into another." In Douglass's reckoning, *he* was the second tub!

In August 1833, after Douglass had been with Thomas and Rowena Auld for just a few months, there was suddenly hope for better days. Master Thomas went to a weeklong Methodist meeting. "If he has got religion," Douglass thought, "he will emancipate his slaves; or, if he should not do so much as this, he will at any rate behave toward us more kindly." But sadly, while Auld found God, he did not change as a slaveholder. He and his wife prayed and sang religious hymns twice a day. They entertained preachers and liberally fed their guests, "all living on the fat of the land," Douglass later remembered, "while we in the kitchen were nearly starving."

Not all the local ministers approved of such treatment. Douglass later wrote fondly of the Reverend George Cookman, "There was not a slave in our neighborhood that did not love and venerate Mr. Cookman." When he visited the Aulds, Cookman called the slaves to prayer and asked about their welfare. He even convinced Samuel Harrison, one of Thomas Auld's neighbors, to free all his slaves. But he could not convince Auld.

Thomas Auld did free one slave, but there was cruelty even in that.

Auld was especially vicious to Henny, the disabled slave his brother had returned to him. Some days he tied her up before breakfast, whipped her "in a manner most brutal and shocking," and left her there until dinner, when he whipped her again. He could not get much work from her, so at last he set her free. Douglass later noted that Auld held on to the slaves who in freedom would have been able to take care of themselves, "turning loose the only cripple among them virtually to starve and die."

The capture of the rebellious Nat Turner

Unlike Henny, Frederick Douglass was a capable worker, but still, he was a problem to Thomas Auld. Again and again, he intentionally let Auld's horse loose, following it to Rowena Hambleton Auld's father's farm, where the slaves were better fed.

In another rebellious act, Douglass and a man named Wilson formed a Sunday school at the home of a free black man in St. Michaels, Maryland. The first reading lesson, with some twenty children, went well. Douglass felt useful. But the second Sunday, the school was broken up by a mob armed with sticks and stones led by three men—Wright Fairbanks, Garrison West, and Thomas Auld. Douglass was warned not to become another Nat Turner, the Virginia slave who two years earlier had started a revolt. If he did, he was told, he would meet the same end as Turner: He would be hanged.

Thomas Auld felt city life had ruined his slave, and he set about to fix that. He decided to send him to Edward Covey, a poor farmer with the reputation of being able to break and train even the most willful slave. On January 1, 1834, with a small bundle of clothes tied to a stick, Frederick Douglass set out on a seven-mile hike to meet his new master.

Covey was a round-shouldered, short-necked, thin, fidgety man who spoke, according to Douglass, out of the side of his mouth in a doglike growl. His workers nicknamed him "the Snake" because he crept and crawled in ditches and gullies and hid behind trees to keep an eye on his workers. Sometimes he pretended to ride off, only to hide and watch his field hands to be sure they were hard at work.

On his third day with Covey, Douglass was told to take a cart and two unruly oxen into the forest and gather firewood. At first, Douglass was able to keep up with the animals, but when they reached the woods, they ran

A slave whipping in New Castle, Delaware

wild and crashed into a tree. Then they became tangled in the brush. At last, Douglass freed the animals and loaded the cart. But on the way back, the oxen got loose again and destroyed a gatepost.

Covey caught up with Douglass. He cut off a few tree shoots and demanded Douglass take off his clothes and prepare to be whipped. When Douglass refused, Covey ran at him and beat him with the tree shoots. At least once a week for the next six months, Covey beat Douglass.

With Covey, the workday began at dawn and ended at best at dark, but sometimes as late as midnight—only to begin again the next morning at dawn. Douglass later wrote, "We worked all weathers. It was never too hot or too cold; it could never rain, blow, snow, or hail too hard for us to work in the field. . . . The longest days were too short for him and the shortest nights were too long for him." Douglass didn't have enough time to eat or sleep, except on Sundays.

He thought of running away. He was willing to die rather than be worked and beaten to death. He even thought of suicide.

One very hot Friday in August, Douglass felt ill in the field. His head ached and he felt dizzy. He fell and then crawled to a shady spot by a fence to rest. When Covey found Douglass, he kicked him and demanded he get up. Douglass tried but couldn't. "If you have got the headache," Covey said, hitting him in the head with a piece of wood, "I'll cure you." The blow tore into Douglass's skin. Blood flowed. Douglass got up and ran off. Covey shouted for him to come back, but what sensible man would return for a sure beating? Douglass went to Thomas Auld, who, he thought, wouldn't "allow his property to be thus bruised and battered, marred and defaced."

He was wrong. Auld didn't believe Douglass was sick, just that he was trying to get out of work. Douglass begged for a new master. He said that if he went back, Covey would surely kill him. But Auld didn't give in. He said that surely Douglass "deserved it." He could stay the night, but the next morning he had to return.

Saturday morning, Douglass walked back. By nine o'clock he had reached Covey's. As he approached the farm, Covey jumped out with a rope and a whip,

Freedom's Journal *was the first African American newspaper published in the United States. It was printed weekly in New York from 1827-1829.*

FREEDOM'S JOURNAL

March 14, 1828

New York, New York

SUMMARY.

NEW COLOURED CHURCH–From our friend Mr. Reymond, we learn that our Coloured brethren in Salem, Mass. are proceeding with a praiseworthy spirit in the erection of a house of Worship; having erected the frame and covered it some time since.

NEW ORGAN.–The Congregation of the Protestant Episcopal Church of St. Thomas, Philadelphia, (Coloured) have lately purchased a neat and elegant Organ for the use of the said Church....

FIRE–The United States (Phil.) Gazette says, that a fire broke out on Saturday evening in the Tract Society's Depository, but by timely discovery and great exertion it was extinguished without much damage.

A man in Georgia recently drank a quart of raw whiskey, and died shortly after. The Coroner's jury returned a more sensible verdict than is usually given by such juries, viz. "premeditated death by Whiskey." ...

EARTHQUAKE–A terrible Earthquake took place in Popayan, in the Republic of Colombia, on the 16th of November, which continued for several days. Nearly every building, in a whole district, was rendered unhabitable–the rivers was choked up and spread over the vallies, forming vast lakes and covering several towns, several hundred persons lost their lives.

STRAW PAPER.–Specimens of paper made from straw, at Col. Magraw's mill, near Meadville, Pa. have been shown at Harrisburg. The paper is somewhat rough, but can be written on without sizeing. It will probably make good wrapping paper.

QUESTIONS To Professing Christians, on the Use of Slave-grown Sugar, Coffee, & WHICH crime is the worst?–1st. That of stealing men, women and children and selling them? or, 2ndly, that of buying these stolen men, &c. and dooming them and their posterity for ever, to a cruel, and hopeless bondage, to interminable and uncompensated toil, (under the lash of the cart-whip) and to moral and intellectual degradation, and the captivity, imprisonment, and death of the soul? or, 3rdly, that of purchasing the produce of their toil, and bribing the "Men-stealers," or sellers, or possessors, by paying them a higher price (two millions annually in bounties,&c*) than for the same commodity produced by free labour? or, 4thly, that of partaking of it when bought by another, whom you have denounced as a criminal for so doing? Is the purchaser any thing less than a receiver of stolen goods?

LETTERS ... It is a well known fact, that black people, upon certain days of public jubilee, dare not to be seen after twelve o'clock in the day, upon the field to enjoy the times; for no sooner do the fumes of that potent devil, Liquor, mount into the brain, than the poor black is assailed like the destroying Hyena or the avaricious Wolf! I allude particularly to the Fourth of July–Is it not wonderful, that the day set apart for the festival of Liberty, should be bused by the advocates of Freedom, in endeavouring to sully what they profess to adore ... A MAN OF COLOUR.

and Douglass ran into the woods. He hid there until nightfall. In the dark, Douglass heard footsteps and buried himself in a pile of leaves. When he peaked out, he saw it was Sandy, an African American slave on his way to visit his wife, a freewoman who lived nearby. Sandy took Douglass to his wife's home, where she fed him and let him stay with them for the night.

"Both seemed to esteem it a privilege to succor me," Douglass later wrote. He was revered by local blacks. "I was the *only* slave *now* in that region who could read and write. . . . My knowledge now was the pride of my brother slaves."

Douglass couldn't stay with Sandy and his wife, and he couldn't run away. The area was almost completely surrounded by water. The strip of land was too narrow for him to be able to escape capture. So the next morning, Douglass returned to Covey.

Covey and his wife were on their way to church. He seemed a changed man, gentle and concerned about Douglass. But the following morning, while Douglass was in the stable feeding the horses, Covey snuck in, grabbed his leg, and threw him to the floor.

This was it! Douglass got what he called the "fighting madness." He later wrote that Covey "was frightened, and stood puffing and blowing, seemingly unable to command words or blows."

They struggled for two hours. At last, Covey gave up the fight and let go. Covey had been bloodied. But, Douglass later wrote, "He had not, in all the scuffle, drawn a single drop of blood from me." After that, Douglass was no longer servile. He even tried to provoke Covey. The next time they fought, he planned to really hurt him. But Covey never again attacked young Frederick Douglass.

Chapter Five ✳

"YOU RASCAL!"

How can I expect to succeed?
I have no knowledge of distance or direction—
I know that Pennsylvania is a free state,
but I know not where its soil begins, or where that of Maryland ends.
—James W. C. Pennington, an African American
slave in Maryland, contemplating escape

"Give him a *bad* master," Douglass once observed about slaves, "and he aspires to a *good* master; give him a good master and he wishes to become his *own* master."

Douglass's year of service to a *bad* master, Edward Covey, ended on Christmas Day, 1834. He stayed with Thomas Auld through the New Year and then reported three miles away to William Freeland, a *good* master.

Freeland had, according to Douglass, "some sense of justice and some feelings of humanity." He worked his slaves hard during the day but left their nights free for rest. He allowed them time for their meals and gave them plenty to eat. Nonetheless, Douglass was restless.

Soon after Douglass went to Freeland's, he was, in his own words, "up to my old tricks." By summer, he had started another Sabbath school. Twenty, thirty—at one time, forty—slaves met, first under an oak tree and later in the house of a free black man. In wintertime, when the workdays were shorter, the school met on weekdays as well as Sundays.

The year at Freeland's, 1835, passed easily for Douglass. He was never whipped, and he got along with his fellow slaves. His temporary master was so pleased with him that he bought a second year of his services from Thomas Auld.

Despite his relatively easy situation, Douglass still dreamed of being free. He made a personal vow that before the end of 1836 he would make a real attempt to escape from slavery.

He did.

Six young slaves—Henry and John Harris, who were brothers; Sandy Jenkins; Charles Roberts; Henry Bailey; and Douglass—met at night and on Sundays to plan their escape. They set the date for their run to freedom for Saturday, April 2, the night before Easter. They would steal a large canoe, set it in the Chesapeake Bay, and paddle north.

The week before their break, Douglass forged a pass for each of them, which reads "This is to certify, that I, the undersigned, have given the bearer, John, full liberty to go to Baltimore, to spend the Easter holidays." Douglass signed the passes "W.H."

The men's few clothes were packed. The food for the journey was prepared. They waited nervously. That Saturday morning, Sandy Jenkins told Douglass of a frightening dream he had had in which Douglass was carried off in the claws of a huge bird while smaller birds pecked at him.

Soon after that, Douglass was working in the field when a horn sounded. It was the call to breakfast. As he approached the house, he saw four white men on horseback riding toward him. Walking behind them were two African Americans, bound and tied.

"It is all over with us," Douglass thought. "We were surely betrayed."

"Cross your hands," Douglass and John Harris were told, and they were tied up.

"Cross your hands," Henry Harris was told.

"No, I won't," he answered.

Two of the white men took out pistols.

"Shoot! Shoot me!" Harris cried out. "You can't kill me but once . . . I won't be tied."

Harris swung and knocked the guns from the men's hands. There was a fight, and in the end Harris was beaten, subdued, and tied.

Douglass realized he held one of the forged passes. He quickly threw it into a fire. Luckily, the others were not searched; their passes were not found.

William Freeland's mother, Betsey, pointed at Douglass and shouted, "You devil! It was you that put it into the heads of Henry and John to run away. But for you, you long legged yellow devil, Henry and John would never have thought of running away."

The men were tied behind three horses and pulled barefoot to town. White townsmen called out that the slaves should be hanged, burnt, or at the very least severely whipped. During the interrogation, it became clear that every detail of their plans was known. Douglass and the others suspected that the frightened Jenkins had betrayed them. The escape had failed badly, but Douglass had one consolation. The others in his band did not blame him for what had happened.

A slave being examined before a sale

Douglass was jailed with Henry and John Harris. Henry Bailey and Charles Roberts were jailed, too, but in a separate cell. Jenkins was not arrested, which convinced the others that he had turned them in.

In jail, Douglass was tormented by slave traders who came by to check if his master wanted to sell this strong but rebellious slave. Douglass later wrote, "They laughed, leered, and grinned at us; saying 'Ah! boys, we've got you, haven't we?'" They examined Douglass and the others. They felt their arms and legs and shook their shoulders to see if they were fit and healthy. One of the traders said if he had Douglass, he would quickly cut the devil out of him.

Shortly after Easter, the others were released. But Douglass was kept in prison. He feared that he would be sold to the Deep South, to Georgia, Louisiana, or Alabama, where he would become a human machine working in a cotton field or on a sugar plantation. And from there, escape would be much more difficult.

At last, after a week, Thomas Auld came to free his slave. He threatened to send Douglass to Alabama, but he didn't. Another slaveholder said Douglass was an instigator and threatened to kill him if he was not quickly sent away, so Douglass was returned to Baltimore, to Hugh Auld. There he would be taught a trade. Perhaps to placate the rebellious slave, Thomas Auld promised that if he behaved himself, Douglass would be set free in seven years, when he was twenty-five.

Hugh Auld sent Douglass to work at William Gardiner's shipyard, where seventy carpenters were building two large ships. The demands on Douglass were constant. One man wanted water. Another wanted him to carry some wood, cut it, or get a tool. Douglass had bridled at having one master. Here at the shipyard he had seventy.

Whenever a carpenter was dissatisfied with his work—or sometimes with no provocation whatsoever—he hit Douglass or tried to. Douglass fought back. One day, some eight months after he started at Gardiner's, four of the white carpenters attacked him. They pounded him with their fists, kicked him, and hit him with a metal spike. They left him on the floor, bruised and bloodied. But there was too much fight in Douglass to let it end there. He got up and started after them. Some of the white workers who had watched and even cheered as Douglass was beaten now stopped him. They convinced him it would be impossible to get his revenge on all four men.

Douglass ran home to Sophia Auld, who washed and bandaged him. Her kindness, he later wrote, "was almost compensation for the murderous assault." Her husband was outraged by the attack. He took Douglass to the nearest judge's office and insisted that the four white men be arrested.

"Mr. Auld," the judge asked, "who saw this assault of which you speak?"

Auld told him it was done in front of everyone in the shipyard, but the only one he knew who would testify was Douglass.

"I am sorry," the judge said, "but I cannot move in this matter except upon the oath of white witnesses."

Douglass's battered head was not evidence enough of the beating. "If I had been killed in the presence of a *thousand blacks*," Douglass later wrote, "their testimony combined would have been insufficient to arrest a single murderer."

After that incident, Douglass stopped working at Gardiner's. Hugh Auld, who was now the foreman at Walter Price's shipyard, took Douglass there to seal ships with caulk. Douglass worked at other yards, too. At the end of each week, whatever he earned was given to Auld.

Douglass felt he was being robbed and again thought of escape. He needed money and a plan. It was a common practice in Baltimore and elsewhere for some slaves to be allowed to hire themselves out. The slave would agree to pay his slaveholder a specified amount each week. Whatever he earned over that amount was his to keep.

In the spring of 1838, Thomas Auld came to Baltimore to buy supplies. Douglass spoke with him, but Auld refused to let him hire out and warned Douglass that if he ran away, he would do whatever was necessary to get him back. "Lay out no plans for the future," Auld said. "If you behave yourself properly, I will take care of you."

The talk didn't dissuade Frederick Douglass.

Two months after Thomas Auld had returned home, Douglass asked Hugh Auld if he could hire out, and a deal was made. Douglass would pay for his own food, clothing, and caulking tools and work for whomever he wanted. From his pay he would give Hugh Auld three dollars a week. It was a hard bargain. With all his expenses, he would have to earn at least six dollars a week just to break even. And work was uncertain. In bad weather, there might be no work at all. Still, Douglass hoped he could save one or two dollars each week and eventually buy his freedom.

Every Saturday night, Douglass made his weekly payment to Auld. But one Saturday, after his workday was done, he went away with friends. He returned late the next day and paid Auld.

"You rascal! I have a great mind to give you a severe whipping," Auld said. "How dare you go out of the city without first asking and obtaining permission? . . . The next thing I shall hear of, will be your running away."

After this, Auld refused to let Douglass hire himself out. He expected

Douglass to find work, but everything he earned would go to Auld. This ended Douglass's hope of saving enough money to buy his freedom.

When Monday came, Douglass didn't go out and look for work. He didn't work all week. On Saturday night he had no wages to hand over, and Auld was furious. He promised to find Douglass plenty of work. And Douglass promised himself he would work for Auld for just three more weeks and that on Monday, September 3, 1838, he would run north to freedom.

With his mind set to escape, Douglass found the work tolerable. The next week he earned nearly nine dollars, a good sum for the time, and on Saturday he gave it all to Hugh Auld. He worked the following week and earned a full nine dollars, and on Saturday he gave it to Auld. "So well pleased was he," Douglass later wrote, "that he gave me twenty-five cents! and 'bade me make good use of it.'" Douglass would use it to help finance his escape.

As the date of his escape neared, Douglass thought of the many people he would never see again. He was not thinking of family—he had none in Baltimore. But he had many friends.

Anna Murray

One of his friends was Anna Murray, a free black woman whom he had met at a meeting of the East Baltimore Improvement Society, a charitable and educational organization. Anna Murray worked as a housekeeper for a wealthy family. Douglass and Murray hoped to one day marry. She gave him money to help him run away.

The next week, Douglass worked only four days, Monday through Thursday. The next two days he prepared for his escape. He borrowed a black seaman's papers, documents that described him as a free sailor.

On Saturday, Douglass gave Auld his week's wages—six dollars. As usual, Douglass spent Sunday with his friends. Then on Monday, September 3, 1838, he jumped on the last car of a train bound for Philadelphia. His friend Isaac Rolls threw his bundle of belongings onto the moving train, and Douglass was on his way north, on his way to freedom.

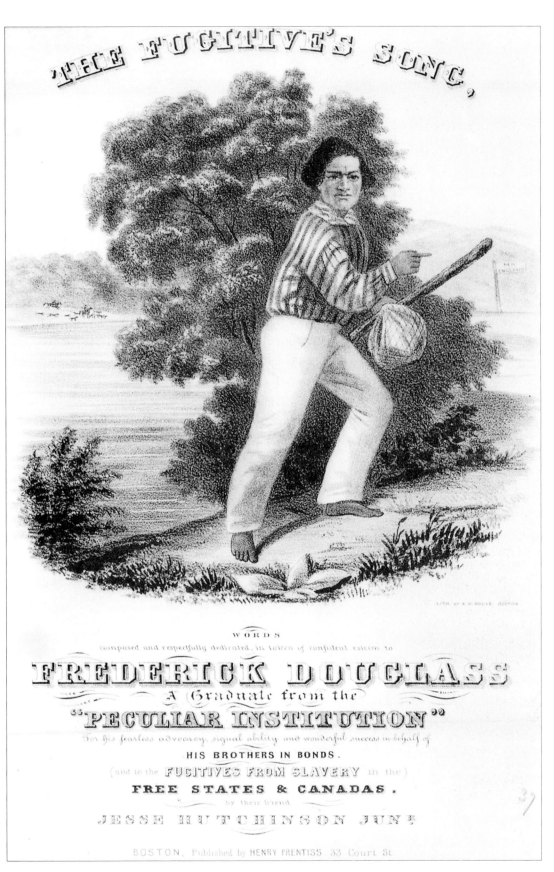

Frederick Douglass, from the cover of the sheet music of a song celebrating his escape published in 1845

Newspaper report, 1835.

A SABBATH SCHOOL BROKEN UP BY A MAGISTRATE.—From the Cincinnati Journal. In Gallatin County, Kentucky, a Sabbath-school was organized for the benefit of slaves. None were encouraged to come, but such as had leave from their masters. About thirty attended, and manifested great anxiety to learn to read the word of God. The school continued five or six Sabbaths without interruption. At length an Esp. constable and about twenty-five others came one Sabbath evening; just after the school was closed, and took the two young men, who formed and taught the school, with a warrant, and fined them sixteen shillings each, and costs for holding an unlawful assembly. The law under which the fine was infected, order twenty lashes on the bare back well laid on, in case the fine is not promptly paid. From the warrant it appeared that a good colonizationist was the informant. This fact shows that slavery tends not only to oppress the colored slave, but even the white freeman. These two benevolent young men, had they been unable to tender their fine, might have received twenty lashes each, on the bare back, well laid on. This shows us how much hope there is of preparing the mass of slaves for freedom, when even Sabbath-schools are broken up by the civil magistrates.!! For gradual emancipation there is just one argument, and that is, the avarice of the master. The slaves, as a mass, never can be educated in a state of slavery. Avarice, the sole reason for slavery, will neither yield up either the time or expense necessary to educate slaves. Those who are willing to educate their own slaves will not be allowed to do it. The above fact is susceptible of the clearest proof. JOHN RANKIN, Ripley, Brown County, Ohio. October 24, 1835.

Chapter Six

NEW BEDFORD: "I HAD NO MASTER"

Brethren, arise, arise! . . .
You cannot suffer greater cruelties than you have already.
Rather die freemen than live to be slaves.

—FROM AN 1843 SPEECH IN BUFFALO, NEW YORK,
BY THE REVEREND HENRY H. GARNET,
WHO ESCAPED SLAVERY AT THE AGE OF ELEVEN

Douglass was frightened. His only hope of escape was that no official would take a careful look at his borrowed papers. They were legitimate—but clearly not his. At the top was a picture of an American eagle. Below that was a description of the free sailor who owned the papers: his name, age, color, height, and any birthmarks or scars. The man described looked nothing like Frederick Douglass.

An 1840s train

Douglass dressed like a sailor in a red shirt, a sailor hat, and a black scarf tied loosely around his neck. To avoid the ticket seller, who would surely check his papers, he boarded the train just as it was leaving the station and sat in the car set aside for blacks.

The train was already several miles outside Baltimore when the conductor entered the car. He checked the papers of a few of the other passengers. Then he came to Douglass.

"I suppose you have your free papers?"

"Yes sir," Douglass answered. "I have a paper with the American eagle on it, and that will carry me round the world."

The train was noisy and crowded. The conductor took a quick look at the papers, collected the fare, and walked on. Douglass was safe for now, but he was still in Maryland. He would be truly free only when he traveled through neighboring Delaware, also a slave state, and made it into Pennsylvania.

At the Susquehanna River Douglass boarded a ferry. One of the deckhands, an African American named Nichols, asked him lots of questions. Where was he going? When would he return? Douglass quickly got away from him.

A drawing of a fugitive slave from an 1837 issue of an antislavery publication

At the other side of the river he got on a train going north and was soon in danger again. The train stopped beside another train heading south. Captain McGowan, someone who knew Douglass from Walter Price's shipyard, sat by the window just opposite Douglass. If McGowan looked out, he would surely recognize him. Luckily, he didn't look out.

There was also a German blacksmith riding with Douglass. "I really believe he knew me," Douglass later wrote, "but had no heart to betray me."

As he rode to freedom, "minutes were hours, and hours were days." At last, they reached the border separating Delaware from Pennsylvania. This was the part of the journey Douglass feared most, because he knew slave catchers patrolled there.

No one stopped Douglass.

He reached Philadelphia and immediately boarded a train bound for New York and arrived there on Tuesday morning, September 4, 1838. Finally, he felt that the chains of his slavery had been broken.

That good feeling did not last very long.

Douglass soon met William Dixon, a Baltimore runaway known during his slave days as Dr. Allender's Jake. Dixon told him that many Southern whites traveled through the city on the lookout for fugitive slaves, and that even some free blacks might betray him. He advised Douglass not to take work at a shipyard, because if Hugh Auld came after him, that would be the first place he would look.

A scene of New York in 1830

Douglass had no home, no job, no friends, and almost no money. If he had to stay away from shipyards, where he could perhaps get a job as a caulker, he had little hope of finding work.

"I was indeed free—from slavery," Douglass later wrote, "but free from food and shelter as well."

He spent his first two nights as a freeman sleeping in the street. Then, while wandering in a seedy part of the city, he met a sailor who sent him to David Ruggles, a "conductor" on the Underground Railroad, an escape route for runaway slaves with safe stops all the way to Canada. Douglass stayed with Ruggles for several days. While he was there, he sent a message to Anna Murray to join him. On September 15, 1838, soon after she reached New York, they were married by the Reverend J. W. C. Pennington, a Presbyterian minister who was himself a runaway.

Ruggles told Douglass that New Bedford, Massachusetts, would be safer for him than New York. Many of the people who lived in New Bedford were antislavery. And because it was a port and lots of whaling ships were outfitted there, there would be work for him as a caulker. On September 15, just after their wedding ceremony, Douglass and his bride boarded a steamship and traveled overnight to Newport, Rhode Island, where they boarded a stagecoach for New Bedford.

They had no money to pay the stagecoach driver, so when they arrived in New Bedford, the driver kept their baggage until their fares were paid. Ruggles had given Douglass the name of a place to go, the home of Mary and Nathan Johnson, a wealthy African American couple. The Johnsons paid the fares and welcomed the Douglasses into their home. Nathan Johnson assured Douglass that he was safe in New Bedford, that the local antislavery activists would not allow a runaway to be captured and sent back.

To make himself more difficult to find, Douglass had changed his name from Bailey to Johnson. But his host now told him that the name "Johnson" was much too common, that he should change it again. He suggested "Douglass," from the Scottish author Sir Walter Scott's narrative poem *The Lady of the Lake*. So Frederick Bailey, who had been born a slave, became a freeman named Frederick Douglass.

Douglass was amazed when Nathan Johnson told him there was nothing in the laws of Massachusetts to prevent an African American man from becoming governor, and that black and white children went to the same public schools. Douglass later wrote, "I could have landed in no part of the United States where I should have found a more striking and gratifying contrast."

The affluence of New Bedford was also revelation to him. He had been taught that slavery created wealth, so he had expected people in free states, who did not have slaves, would be poor. But he found that some working-class people in this Massachusetts town lived better than many slaveholders on the Eastern Shore of Maryland. In fact, many free African Americans in New Bedford had sinks, drains, machines for wringing clothes, and many other "modern" devices, and lived better than some poor slaveholders.

The wharves there were quieter than the ones in Baltimore, with no loud singing, cursing, or fighting, just the efficient loading and unloading of ships. Douglass found "everything managed with a much more scrupulous regard to economy, both of men and things, time and strength." Five or six Northerners with the help of an ox could do the work of twenty or thirty Southern workers.

Douglass put on laborer's clothes and walked toward the wharves to find work. On his way he saw a large pile of coal in front of the house of the Reverend Ephraim Peabody. He went to the kitchen door and asked Mrs. Peabody if he could bring in the coal. "What will you charge?" she asked. Douglass answered, "I will leave that to you, madam." He quickly brought in the coal and was paid two silver half-dollars.

His heart "swelled" as he held the money, "realizing," he later wrote, "that I had no master who could take it from me, that it was mine, that my hands were my own, and could earn more of the precious coin."

Douglass found work loading a ship. But when he took a job as a caulker, the whites refused to work with him. Slavery was outlawed in New Bedford, but prejudice and discrimination were not.

Douglass took whatever jobs he could get. He cut wood; shoveled coal; dug cellars; loaded, unloaded, and scrubbed ships. Then he worked in a brass foundry, where he sometimes operated the bellows, a device he had to pump to direct air into the foundry's furnace. When he did this job, he often nailed a newspaper to a post and read while he worked.

Douglass's favorite was *The Liberator,* an antislavery weekly newspaper edited by William Lloyd Garrison, a white abolitionist. "It detested slavery—exposed hypocrisy and wickedness in high places," he later wrote, "made no truce with the traffickers in the bodies and souls of men; it preached human brotherhood, denounced oppression, and, with all the solemnity of God's word, demanded the complete emancipation of my race." Douglass called its editor "the man—the Moses, raised up by God, to deliver his modern Israel from bondage."

Douglass was a religious man. In New Bedford, he joined the mostly white Elm Street Methodist Church. But it was a segregated congregation, and at communion he felt humiliated when he and the few other blacks were served last. He tried other churches and at last settled on the African Methodist Episcopal Zion Church.

When she could, Anna Murray Douglass worked as a housekeeper. But often she was busy at home. Frederick and Anna Douglass would have five children—three sons and two daughters: Rosetta, Lewis Henry, Frederick Jr., Charles Remond, and Annie.

February 5, 1831

Boston, Massachusetts

PRISON ANECDOTE.

I will give the public an anecdote, showing in what manner a slaveholder can reason. During my late incarceration in Baltimore prison, four men came to obtain a runaway slave. He was brought out of his cell to confront his master, but pretended not to know him—did not know that he had ever seen him before—could not recollect his name. Of course, the master was exceedingly irritated. 'Don't you remember,' said he, 'when I gave you, not long since, thirty-nine lashes under the apple-tree? Another time, when I gave you a sound flogging in the barn? Another time, when you was scourged for giving me the lie, by saying that the horse was in a good condition?'

'Yes,' replied the slave whose memory was thus quickened, 'I do recollect. You have beaten me cruelly without a cause; you have not given me enough to eat and drink; and I don't want to go back again. I wish you to sell me to another master—I had rather even go to Georgia, than to return home.'

'I'll let you know, you villain,' said the master, 'that *my* wishes, and not *yours*, are to be consulted. I'll learn you how to run away again.'

The other men advised him to take the black home, and cut him up in inch pieces for his impudence, obstinacy and desertion—swearing tremendously all the while. The slave was ordered back to his cell.

I had stood speechless during this singular dialogue, my blood boiling in my veins, and my limbs trembling with emotion. I now walked up to the gang, and addressing the master as calmly as possible, said

'Sir, what right have you to that poor creature?' He looked up in my face very innocently, and replied

'My father left him to me.'

'Suppose,' said I, 'your father had broken into a bank, and stolen ten thousand dollars, and safely bequeathed the sum as a legacy could you conscientiously keep the money? For myself, I had rather rob any bank to an indefinite amount than kidnap a fellow being, or hold him in bondage: the crime would be less injurious to society and less sinful in the sight of God.'

The man and his crew were confounded. What! To hear such sentiments in Maryland,—and in jail, too!

IMPORTANT FROM EUROPE.

[Lo]ndon papers to Dec. 19th, inclu[siv]e, have been received at New [Yor]k, bringing the highly important [int]elligence of a *Revolution in [Pol]and* and the flight of the Grand [Du]ke Constantine to Russia! The [rev]olt appears to have been led on, [lik]e that of Paris, by the lads of the [mi]litary school. Forty-one Colonels [and] Majors were killed in endeavor[in]g to keep the troops in obedience. [I]t is added that two Aide-de-[ca]mps of the Grand Duke were [als]o slain.

[I]t is stated that a new revolution [ha]s commenced in Prussia.

[P]ope Pius VIII. Died in Novem[be]r of gout in the stomach.

[M]r. O'Connell was busy in [bri]nging forward the subject of dis[sol]ving the Legislative Union of [Ire]land with England and Scot[la]nd.

London,—There is a report in the [ci]ty, which has obtained some [cr]edit, to the effect that a great [ba]ttle had taken place between the [Pol]es and the Russians in the neigh[bor]hood of Warsaw. Ten thousand [m]en are said to have perished, and [th]e Poles are supposed to have been [vic]torious. The Emperor Nicholas, it is added, is about to take command of the army in person. —*Dec. 17.*

A NEW-YORK NEGRO AND A KENTUCKIAN

Not long since, a gentleman from Kentucky was standing at the door of one of our hotels whence he was about staring for the steamboat. Wishing for some one to carry his baggage, and seeing a spruce looking negro passing along the street, he called out to him— 'Here, you nig, take my trunk and carry it down to the steamboat.'

The negro stopped, and raising his quizzing glass to his eye, stared at the Kentuckian with a mistune of indignation and astonishment. Having scanned him sufficiently with his glass, he gave his hat an independent twist to one side, pulled up his dickey about his ears, drew himself up to his fullest height, and thus replied, 'Did you 'dress that language to me, sir?' 'Yes, you black rascal; I want you to take my trunk to the boat.' 'Indeed! I guess you come from the slave holding states, didn't you, if I may take the liberty to ax?'

'Ay, you black dog—and what if I did? You take too much liberty, I can tell you.' 'Why, I was sure you must have come from the slave states, otherwise you wouldn't treat a gentleman in this *supersilly* manner, just because his skin isn't of the same color as your own.'

'Shut up your thick lips, or I'll stick my fist down your throat.' 'We don't have any gag laws in this state.' 'Well, you ought to have, to stop the mouths of such saucy black rascals as you are. I wish I had you in Kentucky once.'

'I suppose you'd *gouge* me then. But, thank heaven, I'm not in Kentucky, and not a slave, neither. And what's more, I undertake to tell you Mr. *impotence*, that there's no *gouging*, no gagging in this free state, and one man is as much *inspected* as another, if he behaves as well, although he is a blackman, or a Nig as you call him. Behavior makes the man, sir. For my part, I should be ashamed to show my face among other gentlemen, if I 'dressed a man in the *supersilly* manner you did me.'

Having finished his speech, the dark colored beau again raised his quizzing glass to his eye, and giving his antagonist a look of ineffable disdain, walked on; while the Kentuckian almost doubting his senses, wondered what sort of republican principle that could be which gives a black man as much liberty as a white one.—*New York Constellation.*

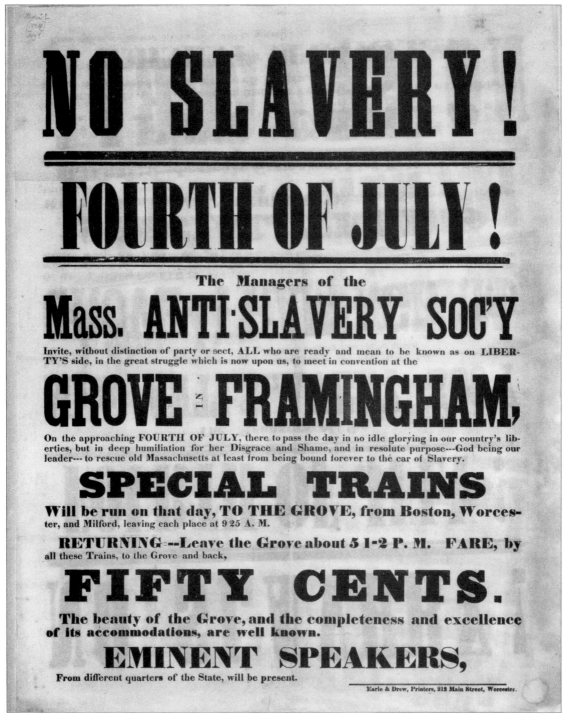

Poster advertising an 1854 rally of the Massachusetts Anti-Slavery Society

THE LECTURE CIRCUIT:
"I CAN TELL YOU WHAT I HAVE SEEN"

Slavery has been made the question of this generation.
—Wendell Phillips, 1853 address
to the Massachusetts Anti-Slavery Society

Frederick douglass was awed by William Lloyd Garrison, the editor of *The Liberator*. He saw in him "the resurrection and the life of the dead and buried hopes" of his enslaved people. He first heard Garrison speak in New Bedford at Liberty Hall, an old, dilapidated building with doors hanging off their hinges and windows broken by stones and rotten eggs thrown to disrupt the many abolitionist meetings held there. "The style of Mr. Garrison's speaking," Douglass said later in a lecture, "would not be called eloquent. There was no fine flow of words, no dazzling sentences formed to tickle the ear. His power was the power which belongs only to character, conviction, and high moral purpose, and which cannot well be counterfeited."

William Lloyd Garrison was born in 1805 in Newburyport, Massachusetts, and trained to be a shoemaker and a cabinetmaker. But at the age of thirteen, he was hired out as the indentured servant of Ephraim W. Allen, the publisher

William Lloyd Garrison

State Street, Boston, in 1840

of the *Newburyport Herald*. Garrison was soon an expert printer, and he began to write anonymous articles for the newspaper.

At twenty, Garrison became editor of the *Newburyport Free Press*, but that newspaper quickly failed. He moved to Boston and was the editor of the *National Philanthropist*, one of the first American newspapers to preach total abstinence from liquor. In 1828, he moved to Bennington, Vermont, where he worked on another newspaper. In 1830, while Douglass was living with the Aulds in Baltimore, Garrison took a job as coeditor of a Baltimore newspaper, the *Genius of Universal Emancipation*, and advocated immediate freedom for all slaves. In one issue he called the owner of a ship used to move slaves from Baltimore to New Orleans a "domestic pirate," was sued, convicted of libel, and jailed for seven weeks.

On January 1, 1831, shortly after he was released from prison, Garrison and his partner, Isaac Knapp, published the first issue of *The Liberator*. For the next thirty-five years, it was the nation's leading abolitionist newspaper.

"I will be as harsh as truth and as uncompromising as justice on this subject," Garrison wrote in the first issue. "I do not wish to think, or speak, or write with moderation—I am in earnest—I will not equivocate—I will not retreat a single inch, and *I will be heard.*"

"Why are you all on fire?" someone asked. Garrison answered, "I have need to be all on fire, for I have mountains of ice about me to melt."

The year *The Liberator* was first published was a pivotal year in the fight against slavery. In 1831, Nat Turner, a Virginia slave, and some sixty of his followers went on a killing spree, taking the lives of more than fifty whites. The rebellion caused a panic among slaveholders and led to a call in the Virginia legislature to end slavery. Supporters of the proposal said that, beyond being unjust and cruel, slavery was chasing free workers from the state and had ruined every industry but agriculture. Lawmakers had only to look to the North to see the profit possible in a free society. The debate went on for several weeks, but in the end nothing was done.

Resentment against *The Liberator* was strong. The governor of Georgia offered a reward of five thousand dollars to anyone who kidnapped Garrison. A local law passed in Georgetown, a section of Washington, D.C., made any free African American caught picking up a copy of the paper at the post office subject to whipping, imprisonment, and possible enslavement. The campaign against his newspaper led to violence and in Boston, in 1835, Garrison was attacked and almost killed by a proslavery mob.

Six years later, Douglass and Garrison crossed paths.

In August 1841, Frederick Douglass traveled to Nantucket, an island about eighty miles from New Bedford, to an antislavery convention organized by Garrison and his associates. The meetings were held in a large square building known as the "Big Shop." Douglass expected to just sit there and listen, but William C. Coffin, a white abolitionist from New Bedford, had heard his story and asked him to speak.

"It was common in anti-slavery meetings," according to a contemporary report, "for fugitives, in their broken, illiterate way, to tell of their suffering, that northern men and women might know the character of Negro slavery."

Douglass stood before the mostly white audience and spoke with "the utmost difficulty," he wrote later, hardly able to utter "two words without hesitation and stammering." He apologized for his shortcomings as a speaker. He explained that slavery was a poor school for a young man's head and heart. Then he told of his family, his history as a slave, and his escape.

"In a few moments his fear of his audience vanished," according to the contemporary report, "and he poured forth a torrent of burning eloquence, such as the majority present never before had heard. His voice and action were natural, his language was intensely eloquent, and his whole bearing that of a great orator. The audience was astounded; it seems almost miraculous, that an ignorant slave should possess such powers."

Garrison followed Douglass to the podium. He declared that the great orator Patrick Henry of the American Revolution had never spoken more eloquently for liberty than had Douglass. Then he called out a question. "Have we been listening to a thing, a piece of property, or to a man?"

"A man! A man!" the audience of some five hundred people replied.

"And should such a man be held a slave in a republican and Christian land?"

"No, no! Never, never!"

"Shall such a man ever be sent back to slavery from the soil of old Massachusetts?"

At that point, almost everyone in the hall jumped to his feet and shouted, "No, no!"

"I shall never forget his first speech at the convention," Garrison later wrote. "The extraordinary emotion it excited in my own mind—the applause which followed from the beginning to the end of his felicitous remarks. I think I never hated slavery so intensely as at that moment."

Douglass's speech was so effective that he was offered a job. John A. Collins, director of the Massachusetts Anti-Slavery Society, asked him to become a full-time lecturer. Douglass didn't think he was suited to be a professional speaker. He thought he should continue to work as a laborer. Some of his African American friends warned that publicly declaring himself to be a former slave was announcing his low status and that admitting he was a runaway would lead to his recapture. Still, Douglass believed strongly in the cause of abolition and agreed to work for the society. But with the advice of his friends in mind, he would not reveal in his lectures where he was born, the name he was known by as a slave, or the name of his slaveholder.

The society would pay him a salary. With the promise of a steady income, he moved his family some seventy miles to the north, to Lynn, Massachusetts, only a short train ride from Boston, where Garrison and many other leaders of the abolition movement lived. From Lynn, Douglass traveled across New England and the middle states—Massachusetts, New Hampshire, Rhode Island, New York, Ohio, Indiana, and Illinois.

When Douglass stood to speak, he impressed his audience. He was tall, broad-shouldered, and handsome, "a commanding person," according to the editor of a New Hampshire abolitionist newspaper, and "cut out for a hero." When he spoke, his voice was "highly melodious and rich, and his enunciation quite elegant." The editor of a Massachusetts newspaper, the *Hingham Patriot*, wrote that Douglass talked "as men who have spent all their lives over books . . . and considering the poor advantages he must have had as a slave, he is certainly a remarkable man."

"He had just escaped from the 'house of bondage,'" one listener wrote, "and as he recited his experience as a slave, his sufferings as he grew old enough to realize the bitterness of his lot . . . his eyes would now flash with defiance, and grow dim with emotions he could not control." When he lowered his voice, "notes trembled on his tongue."

"It has rarely been my lot to listen to one whose power over me was greater than Douglass," one Massachusetts man wrote to Garrison, "and not over *me* only, but over all who heard him."

Douglass was introduced to his audiences as a "thing—a piece of Southern property," and for the first few months he spoke only of his experiences as a slave. But he grew bored telling the same stories again and again. He felt a need to not simply describe slavery, but to denounce it.

"I feel greatly embarrassed when I attempt to address an audience of white people," he said in a speech in October 1841 in Lynn. "I am not used to speak to them, and it makes me tremble when I do so, because I have always looked up to them with fear. My friends, I have come to tell you something about slavery—what I *know* of it, as I have *felt* it. . . . I have suffered under the lash without the power of resisting. Yes, my blood has sprung out as the lash embedded itself in my flesh. And yet my master has the reputation of being a pious man and a good Christian."

In a November 1841 speech before the Plymouth Church Anti-Slavery Society, he said, "People in general will say that they like colored men as well as any other, *but in their proper place*. They assign us that place. They will not allow that we have a head to think and a heart to feel and a soul to aspire. They treat us not as men, but as dogs. . . . You degrade us and then ask why we are degraded. You shut our mouths and then ask why we don't speak. You close your colleges and seminaries against us and then ask why we don't know more."

Douglass was a powerful speaker, and people came to antislavery meetings just to hear him. When he spoke first, some people listened to him and then left. When he spoke last, they waited until the end of the program just to hear him.

Douglass was determined to fight the spirit of slavery wherever he found it. Once, when he was traveling with a friend, James N. Buffum, a white abolitionist, they boarded the Eastern Railroad bound for Newburyport. The conductor asked Douglass what he was doing in a whites-only car. Douglass replied that he was traveling to Newburyport. The conductor ordered him to leave the car. Douglass refused. The conductor called a few burly railroad workers to forcibly move him. They grabbed Douglass, and he grabbed his seat. Although Douglass was removed from the whites-only car, so was his seat.

Whenever his friend the white abolitionist Wendell Phillips was with him and Douglass was moved to the car for African Americans, Phillips followed him. "Douglass, if you cannot ride with me," he said, "I can ride with you." Phillips also refused to eat in any restaurant that would not serve his friend Frederick Douglass.

In September 1843, in Richmond, Indiana, Douglass was pelted with eggs. At another Indiana meeting, the Reverend George Bradburn, an elderly man, was warned that there were plans to force Douglass from the platform and to tar and feather him. Then, just after he was warned, some white ruffians approached the speaker's stand.

"What can I do for you, gentlemen?" Bradburn asked.

"We don't want nothing from you."

"Beg your pardon, gentlemen, but I am very deaf," Bradburn said. "Please speak a little louder."

"We want Fred Douglass."

Bradburn cupped his hand by his ear and asked, "What do you say, please?"

All the talk gave Douglass time to escape.

In Pendleton, Indiana, Douglass stood ready to speak when a mob armed with clubs and guns started to tear the platform down. They were about to attack Douglass when Rebecca Fussell, a brave abolitionist, stood between them with her baby in her arms. That stopped the mob. But later a fight broke out in another part of the hall, and Douglass's right hand was broken.

Douglass spoke out against both slavery in the Southern states and

Wendell Philips

A drawing of Frederick Douglass fighting the mob in Indiana, from an 1881 edition of The Life and Times of Frederick Douglass

prejudice in the North. In May 1844, he was one of more than two hundred abolitionists to sign a petition stating that every abolitionist should secede from the United States. Their slogan was "No union with slaveholders." Some abolitionists wanted slaves sent to Africa or Central America and freed there. Douglass wanted them to be set free in the United States.

Douglass was extremely well read, and it showed. He didn't look, talk, or act like a slave; indeed, some people doubted he had ever lived south of the free state of Pennsylvania. It was reported in an 1844 issue of *The Liberator* that, when Douglass spoke, "many persons in the audience seemed unable to credit the statements which he gave of himself, and could not believe that he had actually been a slave. How a man, only six years out of bondage, and who had never gone to school a day in his life, could speak with such eloquence—with such precision of language and power of thought—they were utterly at a loss to devise."

After he spoke, Douglass walked down the aisles of churches and halls and heard people say, "He's never been a slave, I'll warrant you."

The comments rankled him, and in response, in a speech on May 6, 1845, in New York City's large Broadway Tabernacle, a Congregationalist church, he gave details of his enslavement.

I can tell you what I have seen with my own eyes, felt on my own person, and know to have occurred in my own neighborhood. . . . I am not from any of those States where the slaves are said to be in their most degraded condition; but from Maryland, where Slavery is said to exist in its mildest form; yet I can stand here and relate atrocities which would make your blood boil at the statement of them. I lived on the plantation of Col. Lloyd, on the eastern shore of Maryland. . . . I mention the name of this man, and also the persons who perpetuated the deeds which I am about to relate, running the risk of being hunted back into interminable bondage—for I am yet a slave. . . . I will mention the names, and glory in running the risk. . . . We had on the plantation an overseer, by the name of Austin Gore, a man who was highly respected as an overseer—proud, ambitious, cruel, artful, obdurate. Nearly every slave stood in the utmost dread and horror of that man.

Douglass spoke of beatings and of the senseless murder of Bill Denby. He implored the audience to stop supporting a constitution that allows slavery. "While you continue in the Union," he said, "you are as bad as the slaveholder."

It was a powerful speech but also a dangerous one. He was no longer hiding behind an assumed name. Soon his autobiography, *Narrative of the Life of Frederick Douglass,* would be published, and in it would be names and locations—all but how he had escaped. He didn't want to do anything that might prevent other slaves from using his tactics to get free.

Shortly before his autobiography was published, Wendell Phillips wrote to Douglass: "Some years ago, when you were beginning to tell me your real name and birthplace, you may remember I stopped you, and preferred to remain ignorant of all. With the exception of a vague description, so I continued till the other day, when you read me your memoirs. . . . There is no single spot, however narrow or desolate, where a fugitive slave can plant himself and say, 'I am safe.' The whole armory of Northern law has no shield for you. I am free to say that, in your place, I should throw the manuscript into the fire."

Frederick Douglass

NARRATIVE

OF THE

LIFE

OF

FREDERICK DOUGLASS,

AN

AMERICAN SLAVE.

WRITTEN BY HIMSELF.

BOSTON:
PUBLISHED AT THE ANTI-SLAVERY OFFICE.
No. 25 CORNHILL
1845.

Frontispiece and title page from Frederick Douglass's autobiography, published in 1845

"FROM HOUSE TO HOUSE,
AND FROM HEART TO HEART"

Go where we may, we will find American prejudice,
or at least the odor of it, to contend against.

—Dr. James McCune Smith,
an African American physician speaking
at a New York City conference in 1855

"My readers will be delighted to learn," Garrison reported in the May 30, 1845, edition of *The Liberator*, "that Frederick Douglass—the fugitive slave—has at last concluded his *narrative*. All who know the wonderful gifts of friend Douglass know that his *narrative* must, in the nature of things, be written with great power. It is so indeed. It is the most thrilling work which the American press ever issued—*and the most important*. If it does not open the eyes of this people, they must be petrified into eternal sleep." The book "will run through this nation from house to house, and from heart to heart."

The book, *Narrative of the Life of Frederick Douglass*, was a 125-page autobiography that sold for fifty cents. By June, the first American edition was almost sold out, and a new, cheaper one was prepared. It was quickly translated into French and German and was an immediate success in Europe. Within two and a half years, there were eleven thousand copies in print in the United States and thousands more in England, Ireland, France, and Germany.

The many details Douglass included in his book—his slave name, the plantation where he had been enslaved, and the name of his master—spurred great controversy. Despite the details, some people did not believe an uneducated black man could have written such a literate work. Others claimed the slaveholders mentioned were inaccurately portrayed.

A Maryland man named Thompson sent a series of letters to newspapers in the Northeast declaring Douglass's *Narrative* "to be false." The editor of the abolitionist *Albany Patriot* wrote: "Mr. Thompson will have to produce some better testimony than his own opinion." Thompson then complained that the paper did not consider "the evidence of one respectable white man as creditable as the assertions of a ranting negro." And he sent along the testimony of James Dawson, Thomas Graham, and Thomas Auld.

"I have seen and read a *Narrative* of the life of negro Frederick Douglass," James Dawson of St. Michaels, Maryland, wrote, "purporting to have been written by himself, (doubtful) in which that character of Mr. Thomas Auld is most fully aspersed." Dawson claimed to have lived with the Auld family and declared Douglass's book to be a "villainous fabrication."

Thomas Graham, also of St. Michaels, wrote that Auld was his neighbor and that "the statements of Frederick Douglass respecting Mr. Auld's treatment to them, is, in every word, most basely false." Graham claimed Auld's "servants" were well fed and well clothed, and that Auld was more an indulgent father to them than a master.

"He states that I used to flog and starve him," Thomas Auld wrote in a letter to *The Liberator*, "but I can put my hand upon my Bible, and with clear conscience swear that I never struck him in my life, nor caused any person else to do it."

Douglass's response was brilliant. He pointed out that the letters proved his claims. Douglass first thanked Thompson for dispelling all the rumors that he was an imposter, a free black who had never been south of the Pennsylvania-Maryland border. "I am greatly indebted to you," Douglass wrote, "for silencing those truly prejudicial insinuations." He continued, "I can easily understand that you sincerely doubt if I wrote the *narrative*; for if anyone had told me, seven years ago, I should ever be able to write such a one, I should have doubted as strongly as you do now. You must not judge me now by what I then was—a change of circumstances has made a surprising change in me. Frederick Douglass the *freeman* is a very different person from Frederick Bailey the slave." Then he assailed laws in slave states that did not provide equal protection to people of all races.

Publishing the many details of his enslavement put Douglass's freedom in jeopardy. If he were caught, he could be put in chains and sent back to Maryland and bondage. So plans were made for him to go Europe.

Douglass couldn't pay for his passage, so money was raised by his friends, and on August 16, 1845, he boarded the steamer *Cambria*. He traveled with his friend James N. Buffum of Lynn, Massachusetts, a carpenter and an abolitionist. Douglass's wife, Anna, and their children stayed home. He hoped royalties from his book would be enough to support them.

The *Cambria* was a British ship, and though at the time England was more enlightened than America, blacks, including Douglass, had to travel in steerage—the most cramped, least comfortable of the boat's accommodations. "The insult was keenly felt by my white friends," he later wrote, "but to me such insults were frequent, and expected, that it was of no great consequence whether I went in the cabin or in steerage."

As the ship neared Liverpool, England, some passengers and the captain asked Douglass to give one of his famous lectures. Douglass complied and talked about ships like the *Cambria* that at one time transported people in chains from Africa to be sold as slaves. Then there was trouble. Several young men from Georgia and Louisiana interrupted his speech with threats to throw him overboard. The captain stopped it all with threats of his own to put the young men in irons.

A few days after reaching Liverpool, Douglass and Buffum sailed to Ireland and visited Dublin, Cork, and Belfast. Douglass spoke at more than fifty meetings in Ireland and had a hero's welcome wherever he went. "I can truly say," he wrote to Garrison, "I have spent some of the happiest days of my life since landing in this country." He found in Ireland "the entire absence of everything that looks like prejudice against me, on account of the color of my skin."

He traveled through England, Scotland, and Wales, and spoke not only of the horrors of slavery, but also in favor of peace and the rights of women and the evils of alcohol.

In August 1846, William Lloyd Garrison arrived in England. He and Douglass traveled together and lectured at various meetings.

In November, Garrison was set to return to America. By now, Douglass had been away from his family and country for more than a year and wanted to sail with him. He wrote to a friend and asked if it would be safe for him to come home. "Would master Hugh stand much chance in Mass.? Think he could take me from the old Bay State? The old fellow is evidently anxious to get hold of me."

But the law was clear. Douglass still "belonged" to the Aulds. So his friends Anna and Ellen Richardson of Newcastle, England, collected £150 (about $725) and bought his freedom. Like so much in his life, this stirred controversy. Some people were shocked that Douglass would allow his freedom to be bought. They felt it violated antislavery principles because it seemed to acknowledge that one person could own another. The emancipated Douglass simply answered, "I acted from necessity."

On March 30, 1847, "upwards of 400 persons of great respectability," according to a London newspaper, gave him a farewell dinner in London. "Mr. Douglass visited this country," George Thompson, the chairman of the evening, said in his opening remarks, "not only accredited by abolitionists of all parties, but as one of the most efficient laborers in the cause. . . . Highly gifted as he was, he had attracted wherever he went large audiences, and awakened thousands to a sense of their duty."

Thompson's remarks were often interrupted by cheers for Douglass.

"One word as to the general question of slavery," Thompson said. He reminded his audience that while slavery was outlawed in England, there were slaves not only in the United States but also in Brazil, and in the colonies of Spain, France, and Holland.

A few days later, Douglass returned to Liverpool. He was prepared to board the *Cambria*, the same ship he had sailed on when he came to England, when he was told that, once again, he would have to travel in steerage. The euphoria he had felt at his farewell dinner was lost. "I have traveled in this country nineteen months, and have always enjoyed equal rights with other passengers," he wrote in a letter of protest to the *London Times*, "and it was not until I turned my face toward America, that I met with anything like proscription on account of my color."

His letter was picked up by many British newspapers. "Pro-Slavery Persecution in England" and "Disgraceful Prejudice Against a Man of Color" were the headlines of just two of many editorial protests. The British-owned shipping line was quick to respond that nothing like that would happen again on its steamships.

On April 20, 1847, Douglass arrived back in Boston.

He had left Boston a runaway slave. He returned a truly free man. And the great success he had abroad had made him famous at home.

Boston Harbor in 1840

LITH. OF F. PALMER & CO. 98 NASSAU STREET. N.Y.

The Broadway Tabernacle where Douglass first publicly gave the details of his enslavement

"WHAT, TO THE AMERICAN SLAVE, IS YOUR 4TH OF JULY?"

You, like myself, belong to a disenfranchised class.
> —ELIZABETH CADY STANTON,
> A LEADER IN THE STRUGGLE
> FOR WOMEN'S RIGHTS,
> TO FREDERICK DOUGLASS

ON MAY 11, 1847, the American Anti-Slavery Society had its thirteenth-anniversary meeting in the huge Broadway Tabernacle in New York City. William Lloyd Garrison presided over the more than two thousand delegates and officially welcomed Frederick Douglass home. The delegates greeted Douglass with loud and long applause.

"I am here," Douglass said, "a simple man, knowing what I have experienced in slavery, knowing it to be a bad system, and desiring, by all Christian means, to seek its overthrow."

His speech was interrupted by the cheers of the appreciative audience. "I have no patriotism," he said. "The institutions of this country do not know me, do not recognize me as a man. . . . The only thing that links me to this land is my family, and the painful consciousness that there are three million of my fellow-creatures, groaning beneath the iron rod of the worst despotism that could be devised."

What he saw as the hypocrisy of a nation founded on the principle of equality and that yet held so many as slaves was best expressed in a speech he made five years later on Monday, July 5, 1852.

Douglass was the keynote speaker at a Fourth of July celebration in Rochester's three-year-old majestic Corinthian Hall. Because Independence Day was on a Sunday, the gathering was delayed until the next day. In a bit of irony at the time, to protest that for slaves the United States was not a land of freedom, some abolitionists and African Americans routinely observed Independence Day on July fifth, one day later than the rest of the nation. Some African Americans refused to celebrate even on the fifth.

The program began with an opening prayer followed by a reading of the Declaration of Independence. Then, it was Douglass's turn.

He stood before the large, mostly white audience. "Mr. President, Friends and Fellow Citizens," he began. "He who could address this audience without a quailing sensation, has stronger nerves than I have."

He reminded his audience of his beginnings. "The fact is, ladies and gentlemen, the distance between this platform and the slave plantation, from which I escaped, is considerable—and the difficulties to be overcome in getting from the latter to the former, are by no means slight. That I am here today is, to me, a matter of astonishment as well as of gratitude."

He spoke about the American Revolution.

"It is the birthday of your National Independence, and of your political freedom."

He said *your*, not *our*. Throughout his speech he distanced himself from the celebration.

"Oppression makes a wise man mad. Your fathers were wise men," he said. "They felt themselves the victims of grievous wrongs." Referring to the Declaration of Independence and the American Revolution he said, "The freedom gained is yours, and you, therefore, may properly celebrate this anniversary."

Then came the fireworks. He asked and answered the question of the day.

"What, to the American slave, is your 4th of July? I answer: a day that reveals to him, more than all the other days in the year, the gross injustice and cruelty to which he is the constant victim. To him, your celebration is a sham; your boasted liberty, and unholy license; your national greatness, swelling vanity; your sounds of rejoicing are empty and heartless; your denunciations of tyrants, brass fronted impudence; your shouts of liberty and equality, hollow mockery; your prayers and hymns, your sermons and thanksgivings, with all your religious parade, and solemnity, are to him mere bombast, fraud, deception, impiety, and hypocrisy—a thin veil to cover up crimes which would disgrace a nation of savages." One can easily imagine the tall, powerful Douglass's voice rising as he read the next line. "There is not a nation on the earth guilty of practices, more shocking and bloody, than are the people of these United States, at this very hour."

Near the end of this two-hour speech he spoke with optimism.

"I do not despair of this country," he said. "'The doom of slavery is certain. I, therefore, leave off where I began, with hope. While drawing encouragement from the Declaration of Independence, the great principles it contains . . . let every heart join in saying it: God speed the year of jubilee."

When he was done, the more than five hundred people in the hall were silent. Then, as Douglass slowly gathered the many pages of his speech, the audience burst into applause. This talk has been called the century's most powerful speech against slavery. It was widely reprinted.

According to an 1859 article in the *New York Tribune*, Douglass was a leading American lecturer. His well-written, best-selling autobiography proved he was also a talented writer.

Anna and Ellen Richardson, the Englishwomen who helped buy Douglass's freedom, raised $2,174 for him to start a newspaper. "In imagination," he later wrote, "I already saw myself wielding my pen as well as my voice in the great work of renovating the public mind, and building up a public sentiment, which should send slavery to the grave."

Garrison and others, however, told Douglass that he was not meant to be an editor. They said there was no need for another abolitionist newspaper that it would compete with *The Liberator.* Douglass, who was insecure because of his limited formal education, wondered if they were right. If he tried and failed, he worried, it would reflect poorly on other African Americans, and "contribute another proof," he wrote, "of the mental deficiencies of my race."

Nonetheless, he decided to go ahead with his newspaper publishing plans. In deference to Garrison and his New England friends, Douglass did not issue his newspaper in Boston but in Rochester, a city by Lake Ontario in western New York, a center of the abolitionist movement and for many years an Underground Railroad stop for runaway slaves. Douglass had stayed there for three months in 1842 while he was on the lecture circuit, and had felt welcome. "I know of no place in the Union," he later wrote, "where I could have located with less resistance, or received a larger measure of sympathy and cooperation."

The name Douglass chose for his newspaper, *The North Star,* had special meaning for the slave community. Runaways had to find their way north, first to free states, and then to Canada to be out of the reach of slave catchers. They found their direction by looking to the nighttime sky for Polaris, the North Star. "Of all the stars in this brave old, *overhanging* sky," Douglass wrote in the first issue of his newspaper, "the North Star is our choice. To thousands, now free in the British dominions, it has been the star of freedom. To millions, now in our boasted land of liberty, it is the star of hope."

The purpose of the paper, Douglass wrote, "will be to attack slavery in all its forms and aspects; advocate universal emancipation; exalt the standard of public morality; promote the moral and intellectual improvement of the colored people; and hasten the day of freedom to the three millions of our enslaved fellow countrymen."

The four-page newspaper was published from an office in downtown Rochester, at 25 Buffalo Street. It came out weekly, every Friday, from December 1847 until 1860, when, because of financial difficulties, it became a monthly; and it continued publication for three more years. It was known for its famous editor, and in 1851 the name of the newspaper was officially changed to *Frederick Douglass' Paper.*

In 1848, the Douglass family moved from Lynn, Massachusetts, to Rochester, New York. Their new home was a small two-story house at 4 Alexander Street. It had a garden and front porch. Douglass "was fortunate in the comfort of his home," Miss Holly, a frequent visitor, wrote, "made so by the nice and able house-keeping of Mrs. Douglass."

Anna Douglass was quiet and practical. She watched the family finances. If there was some large purchase to be made, she figured the cost and decided whether or not the family could afford it. Anna had good reason to budget the family's money. Publishing *The North Star* was costly. The newspaper was constantly in debt because it didn't have enough subscribers, and many of those it did have owed it money. Douglass quickly went through the money that Anna and Ellen Richardson had collected. In 1848, he mortgaged his house in order to pay expenses.

Beside her more cautious nature, Anna had a temperament very different from her husband, "He has a great deal of uncommon sense," Susan B. Anthony, a leader of the women's rights movement who lived in Rochester, wrote, "but his wife has more than her share of common sense." And Anna, like Douglass's beloved grandmother Betsey Bailey, had a "green thumb." She enjoyed working in their garden.

Anna was also less intellectually curious than her husband. Douglass was now traveling in elite circles, with educated men and women, but Anna could hardly read. In 1848, Douglass hired a teacher for her, but she wasn't an able student.

In May 1849, help for the newspaper again came from England. Julia and Eliza Griffiths, two Englishwomen, came to Rochester and moved into the Douglass house. Julia joined the newspaper staff as its business manager. She soon doubled the number of subscriptions and helped pay off the debt. She also worked with Douglass on his speeches.

Frederick Douglass' Paper

THE *object of the NORTH STAR will be* to attack SLAVERY in all its forms and aspects; advocate UNIVERSAL EMANCIPATION; exalt *the* standard *of* PUBLIC MORALITY; promote *the* moral and intellectual improvement *of the* COLORED PEOPLE; and hasten *the* day *of* FREEDOM to *the* THREE MILLIONS *of* our ENSLAVED FEL-LOW COUNTRYMEN.

NORTH STAR .

Of all *the* stars in this " brave old, over-hanging sky," *the NORTH STAR* is our choice. To thousands now free in *the* British dominions it has been *the STAR* OF FREEDOM. To millions, now in our boasted land of liberty, it is *the STAR* OF HOPE. Dark clouds may conceal, but cannot destroy it. Tempests may toss *the* sea—earthquakes convulse *the* globe—and storm-bolts shake *the* sky—it stands as firm as Heaven. Within its meek and twinkling rays, are Faith, Hope and Freedom—cherishing *the* one, indulging *the* other, and endeavoring to gain *the* last for our slavery smitten countrymen.

We have ventured to call our humble sheet by our favorite *Star.* We have been requested to change it, but as yet see no good reason for doing so. *The* Morning *Star* was suggested; *the* Evening *Star* has been named,—but *the* one is too early, and *the* other too late. *The* Midnight *Star* is our election. We are over-shadowed by gloomy clouds, and on a dark and perilous sea. We need *the* Polar Light to guide us into port.

OUR PAPER AND ITS PROSPECTS.

We are now about to assume *the* management of *the* editorial department of a newspaper, devoted to *the* cause of Liberty, Humanity and Progress. *The* position is one which, with *the* purest motives, we have long desired to occupy. It has long been our anxious wish to see, in this slave-holding, slave-trading, and negro-hating land, a printing-press and paper, permanently established, under *the* complete control and direction of *the* immediate victims of slavery and oppression.

Animated by this intense desire, we have pursued our object, till on *the* threshold of obtaining it. Our press and printing materials are bought, and paid for. Our office secured, and is well situated, in *the* centre of business, in this enterprising city. Our office Agent, an industrious and amiable young man, thoroughly devoted to *the* interests of humanity, has already entered upon his duties. Printers well recommended have offered their services, and are ready to work as soon as we are prepared for *the* regular publication of our paper. Kind friends are rallying round us, with words and deeds of encouragement. Subscribers are steadily, if not rapidly coming in, and some of *the* best minds in *the* country are generously offering to lend us *the* powerful aid of their pens. *The* sincere wish of our heart, so long and so devoutly cherished seems now upon *the* eve of complete realization.

It is scarcely necessary for us to say that our desire to occupy our present position at *the* head of Anti-Slavery Journal, has resulted from no unworthy distrust or ungrateful want of appreciation of *the* zeal, integrity, or ability of *the* noble band of white laborers, in this department of our cause; but, from a sincere and settled conviction that such a Journal, if conducted with only moderate skill and ability, would do a most important and indispensable work, which would be wholly impossible for our white friends to do for us.

It is neither a reflection on *the* fidelity, nor a disparagement of *the* ability of our friends and fellow-laborers, to assert what " common sense affirms and only folly denies," that *the* man who has suffered *the* wrong is *the* man to demand redress,—that *the* man STRUCK in *the* man to CRY OUT—and that he who has endured *the* cruel pangs of Slavery is *the* man to advocate Liberty. It is evident we must be our own representatives and advocates, not exclusively, but peculiarly—not distinct from, but in connection with our white friends. In *the* grand struggle for liberty and equality now waging, it is meet, right and essential that there should arise in our ranks authors and editors, as well as orars, for it is in these capacities that *the* ost permanent good can be rendered to ur cause.

Hitherto *the* immediate victims of slav- y and prejudice, owing to various causes, ve had little share in this department of fort: they have frequently undertaken, and most as frequently failed. This latter fact s often been urged by our friends against ur engaging in *the* present enterprise; but, far from convincing us of *the* impolicy of ur course, it serves to confirm us in *the* cessity, if not *the* wisdom of our under- king. That others have failed, is a reason r our earnestly endeavoring to succeed. ur race must be vindicated from *the* nbarrassing imputations resulting from rmer non-success. We believe that what ght to be done, can be done. We say this, no self-confident or boastful spirit, but ith a full sense of our weakness and nworthiness, relying upon *the* Most High r wisdom and strength to support us in ur righteous undertaking. We are not holly unaware of *the* duties, hardships and sponsibilities of our position. We have eas- y imagined some, and friends have not sitated to inform us of others. Many ubtless are yet to be revealed by that fallible teacher, experience. A view of em solemnize, but do not appal us. We ve counted *the* cost. Our mind is made

up, and we are resolved to go forward.

In aspiring to our present position, *the* aid of circumstances has been so strikingly apparent as to almost stamp our humble aspi- rations with *the* solemn sanctions of a Divine Providence. Nine years ago, as most of our readers are aware, we were held as a slave, shrouded in *the* midnight ignorance of that infernal system—sunken in *the* depths of ser- vility and degradation—registered with four footed beasts and creeping things—regarded as property—compelled to toil without wages—with a heart swollen with bitter anguish—and a spirit crushed and broken. By a singular combination of circumstances we finally succeeded in escaping from *the* grasp of *the* man who claimed us as his property, and succeeded in safely reaching New Bed- ford, Mass. In this town we worked three years as a daily laborer on *the* wharves. Six years ago we became a Lecturer on Slavery. Under *the* apprehension of being re-taken into bondage, two years ago we embarked for England. During our stay in that coun- try, kind friends, anxious for our safety, ran- somed us from slavery, by *the* payment of a large sum. *The* same friends, as unexpect- edly as generously, placed in our hands *the* necessary means of purchasing a printing press and printing materials. Finding our- self now in a favorable position for aiming an important blow at slavery and prejudice,

we feel urged on in our enterprise by a sense of duty to God and man, firmly believing that our effort will be crowned with entire success.

LETTER TO HENRY CLAY.

SIR—I have just received and read your Speech, delivered at *the* Mass Meeting in Lexington, Kentucky, 13th November *1847*, and after a careful and candid perusal of it, I am impressed with *the* desire to say a few words to you....

In *the* speech under consideration, you say,

" My opinions on *the* subject of slavery are well known; they have *the* merit, if it be one, of consistency, uniformity and long duration."

The first sentence is probably true. Your opinions on slavery may be well known, but that they have *the* merit of consistency or of uniformity, I cannot so readily admit. If *the* speech before me be a fair declaration of your present opinions, I think I can con- vince you that even this speech abounds with inconsistencies such as materially to affect *the* consolation you seem to draw from this source. Indeed if you are uni- form at all, you are only so in your incon- sistencies.

Henry Clay

The sight of Douglass and the white Griffiths sisters caused talk. In May 1850, in New York City, it caused trouble. When the three walked together after a meeting of the American Anti-Slavery Society, a gang of white rowdies cursed them. They attacked and beat Douglass.

In 1850, Eliza Griffiths married and moved to Canada. After that, Douglass was often seen working and walking with Julia Griffiths. He denied any impropriety, but still, there was gossip, some of it fueled by Garrison. "I am a husband and a father," Douglass wrote in a letter in his own defense.

In 1852, Julia Griffiths moved out of the Douglass home, and in 1855 she returned to England, where she married a clergyman, the Reverend H. O. Crofts.

In 1856, another woman caused gossip. Ottilia Assing, a German writer working in New Jersey, came to Rochester. She had read Douglass's autobiography *My Bondage and My Freedom*, an updated version of *Narrative*, and was eager to meet its author. She sent many articles about America back to Germany, and in them she was always very complimentary of Douglass. On the topic of his lecturing, she wrote that he had spoken over many years "but never repeated himself, nor lost his hold upon his audience." In 1858, she translated *My Bondage* into German, and in her preface she praised Douglass's "cheerfulness and refinement." Assing died in Paris in 1884 and left a trust fund for Douglass "in recognition of his noble labors in the Anti-Slavery cause."

Daniel Webster

The early to mid-1800s, especially the years Douglass was publishing his newspaper, were years of great change. Those years saw a great decline in slavery in other areas of the Americas. Between 1805 and 1831, slavery was abolished in Haiti, Chile, Mexico, and Bolivia. Argentina and Colombia began to gradually free their slaves in 1813 and 1814, respectively. Even in the southern United States, a smaller proportion of whites depended on forced labor. Would the new western territories of the United States be slave or free? If they were free, the delicate balance in Congress would tip against slavery. What would be done with the nation's capital, which was not only open to slavery but was also a huge slave market?

Senators Henry Clay, Daniel Webster, John C. Calhoun, and Stephen A. Douglas brokered what became known as the Compromise of 1850. With this agreement, the citizens of the territories of New Mexico, Nevada, Arizona, and Utah would decide on their own whether to be slave or free. California would join the Union as a free state, and in Washington, D.C., the slave trade would end. Part of the Compromise was the Fugitive Slave Act. Under this law, anyone caught helping a runaway would face six months in jail and a $1,000 fine.

John C. Calhoun

The Fugitive Slave Act was a blow to abolitionists. "If there ever was a time of solemnity for those who wished well to the slave," Douglass said, "that time was now." He declared that in a struggle with a slave catcher, he "would strike him down" as he would a dog. This was a real break with his old views and with those of his mentor William Lloyd Garrison, who felt that slavery could be ended peacefully.

Garrison was angry and dogmatic, yet he was a pacifist—an odd combination. He hated politics and felt the way to end slavery was to convince the guilty to repent. Since the Constitution supported slavery, he reasoned free states should peacefully secede from the Union.

Douglass disagreed with Garrison. He became more of a political activist and supported the Liberty Party, which had as its tenet the abolition of slavery. In June 1851, when *The North Star* and the Liberty Party paper merged, Garrison and his associates claimed that Douglass had sold out.

Stephen A. Douglas

Some abolitionists worried about the Douglass-Garrison feud. In March 1853, Harriet Beecher Stowe, the author of *Uncle Tom's Cabin*, met with Douglass. She tried but was unable to bring Douglass and Garrison together.

The change in Douglass may be partially traced to a meeting he had had in 1847 with John Brown, "whose character and conversation and whose object and aims in life," Douglass later wrote, "made a very deep impression upon my heart and mind." John Brown was born in 1800 in Torrington, Connecticut. He worked as a tanner but was unsuccessful, and with the hope of better prospects, moved often. He was an ardent abolitionist, and wherever he lived he served as an agent of the Underground Railroad. Brown did not believe slavery could end peacefully and told Douglass that slaveholders had "forfeited their right to live."

Douglass's strong conviction in the right of all people to equal freedom and opportunities included women. Soon after he moved to Rochester, the first American women's rights conference was held in nearby Seneca Falls. A women's Declaration of Independence, calling for equal opportunities of education, employment, and property, was read aloud. Among the one hundred men and women who signed the declaration was Frederick Douglass. "Our doctrine is 'Right is of no sex,'" he wrote in a *North Star* editorial in July 1848. "We therefore bid the women engaged in this movement our humble Godspeed."

Despite the presence of many abolitionists and many women's rights advocates in Rochester, the city's schools were segregated. The Douglass children could not attend Public School 15, the one nearest their house. They were assigned to an inferior school across town. Douglass refused to allow his children to participate in such a system. He hired a private teacher for his sons Lewis Henry, Frederick, and Charles Remond. He enrolled his eldest child, nine-year-old Rosetta, in a private girls' school, Miss Lucilia Tracy's Seward Seminary. The principal was an abolitionist, so Douglass was sure Rosetta would be fairly treated.

Rosetta started school, and Douglass went to Ohio to lecture. When he returned home, he discovered that his daughter had been kept away from the other children in a room with just her teacher. She was not even allowed in the yard when the other girls were outside. Douglass complained, and the principal asked the girls and their parents if anyone would object to having Rosetta in their class. One parent objected, and that was enough for Douglass. He removed his daughter from the school.

"We differ in color, it is true (and not much in that respect)," Douglass wrote to the parent who had objected, "but who is to decide which color is more pleasing to God, or more honorable among men? But I do not wish to waste words or argument on one whom I take to be destitute of honorable feeling."

Douglass and others worked to integrate Rochester's schools. By 1857, its public schools were open to children of all races.

Excerpts from:

June 26, 1851

THE HELL OF SLAVERY.

(From the Georgia Constitutionalist, June 14.) FOR SALE.—A first rate man cook will be sold, if early application is made. He is 25 years old, Virginia raised, of good temper, character unimpeachable, and strictly temperate. He understands all kinds of Meat and Pastry Cooking, both in American and French style. I challenge any one to produce his superior as to neatness and despatch. He understands putting up Pickles of all kinds, Preserves and Sweetmeats. An excellent hand to make Ginger Pop, Soda and Mead, Lemon and Spruce Beer, Ice Cream, Custard Pies, &c. In short he is master of his profession. Apply to A. WILSON, Hamburg, S. C.

P.S.—I also have just received from Virginia direct, a small lot of choice NEGROES, consisting of Seamstresses, House Servants, Wagoners, Field Hands, &c., all of which I will sell at prices to correspond with the times, and will keep constantly on hand a good supply of Negroes for sale upon accommodating terms. A.W.

EMANCIPATED SLAVES. —Mr. Corry, a gentleman who has recently been a resident of Lewis County, Missouri, where he has been a slaveholder, has emancipated a family of slaves, and located them in Cedar township, Iowa, about four miles south of Salem, consisting of a man and his wife and eight children, valued at a round sum of eight thousand dollars.

FREDERICK DOUGLASS' PAPER IS PUBLISHED AT 25 BUFFALO STREET, (OPPOSITE THE ARCADE) BY FREDERICK DOUGLASS. TERMS: TWO DOLLARS PER ANNUM, invariably in advance. ADVERTISEMENTS, not exceeding ten lines, inserted three times for ONE DOLLAR, every subsequent insertion, TWENTY-FIVE CENTS. Liberal reductions made on yearly advertisements. ALL COMMUNICATIONS, whether on business of the paper, or for publication, should be addressed (post-paid) to FREDERICK DOUGLASS, Rochester, N. Y.

AN INTERESTING INCIDENT.

We have just had a call from Mr. Francis, a venerable and intelligent colored man, who is now acting as the agent for the Dawn Institute, Canada West. On his journey thither, he spent a few hours at Niagara Falls, where the incident we are about to narrate occurred. One of our high-born slaveholders, accompanied by his wife and children, and having with him that almost indispensable appendage to such a family, a female "chattel" was spending a few days, merrily no doubt at that place.... The slave safely deposited the family, it seems, at the "Cataract," this done, she made her way to the ferry, took the small boat, and a few noble strokes of the ferryman's oars brought her in safety over the turbid waters to the Canada shores; she speedily made her way to the door of a respectable colored man where she was immediately received, sheltered and protected.... The master soon obtained intimation of her flight, and ascertained her new abode; and with all the brazen effrontery of a southern slave driver, he proceeded to the house and demanded an interview with her. The woman very wisely preferred that the interview should be held with a partition between, he upon the ground beneath, she at the window above. Slaveholder. Jane what has prompted you to this behavior? "Chattel." I wanted my freedom, sir. Slaveholder. Have I not always treated you well? What should induce you now to leave me?

"Chattel." I want to be free, sir. Slaveholder. Come, Jane, none of this foolishness, you must go back with me, and you might as well go back first as last for, go back you shall.

"Chattel." Well, indeed, I aint going back, "that's a fact." Slaveholder. What do you think will become of your children? "Chattel." What will you do with my children? God only knows. I spect you'll do with 'em just what you've done with my other children—sell em. My going back won't make no difference, and I aint going back. . . . Finding the woman wholly intractable, the slaveholder began now to curse and rave like a madman. He cursed the abolitionists, he cursed Canada, he cursed the British, and finally he cursed the Queen. The crowd that stood around listened patiently to his cursing, until the profane wretch cursed the British Queen, when a burly Englishman stepped up, and suiting the action to the word, said to the infuriated blasphemer, "Say that again, and I'll knock your teeth down your throat." It was fitly spoken, and worked like a charm. The slaveholder came to his senses; thinking discretion the better part of valor, he smothered his rage, and like a naughty boy when snubbed effectually, shut his mouth and shrank away from the crowd amidst jeers of derision, leaving his "chattel" in the uncontested enjoyment of the rights and dignity of virtuous womanhood.

"F. D." We have during the last three years signed our editorials with the above initials. The custom originated in a desire to remove certain doubts which were most liberally intertwined by the pro-slavery public as to who wrote the leading editorials of the North Star. It had been repeatedly denied that an uneducated fugitive slave could write the English language with such propriety and correctness as those early editorials evinced. Well, we pocketed the compliment to our skill, although at the expense of our veracity; and having won the former, we set about to establish the latter by affixing our initials.—We have followed the custom now more than three years, and hope we have removed all doubts which our signature can possibly remove in this line. We shall now, therefore, dispense with them, and assume fully the right and dignity of an Editor—

Douglass' Rochester home

The shop where the North Star, Douglass' newspaper, was printed

Chapter Ten

"FORESHADOWED A CONFLICT ON A LARGER SCALE"

Whether my time here shall be fifteen months
or fifteen days or fifteen hours,
I am equally prepared to go.

—John Brown, after his capture,
to Governor Henry Wise of Virginia

The city of Rochester is near Lake Ontario. On the other side of the lake is Canada, which was beyond the reach of slave catchers. That's why the city played such an important role in the Underground Railroad, the collection of hiding places and secret routes followed by fugitive slaves, through forests and along rivers, from slave states through free states, all the way north to Canada.

Runaways traveled mostly by night, always on the lookout for slave catchers. During the day, they hid in sheds, farmhouses, and the attics of "safe houses" owned by sympathetic "agents" of the railroad. Each agent directed runaways to the next safe house. For many fugitive slaves, Rochester was the last stop before crossing to safety. The city had several agents, including Amy and Isaac Post, Edward C. Williams, Lindley Moore, William Bloss, and Anna and Frederick Douglass.

The Douglasses kept a large attic room for runaways. It housed as many as eleven at a time, and hundreds in all. In the morning, when Frederick Douglass arrived at his newspaper office, he often found fugitive slaves waiting for him. He quickly hid them. Then he and his sons collected money, food, clothing, and whatever else was needed to "ship a bale of Southern goods" to Canada, his code for helping runaways.

Douglass wrote many years later about his work on the Underground Railroad. "As a means of destroying slavery, it was like an attempt to bail out the ocean with a teaspoon, but the thought that there was *one* less slave, and one more freeman—having been myself a slave—brought my heart unspeakable joy." Of his efforts for the railroad, he wrote: "I can say, I never did more congenial, attractive, fascinating, and satisfactory work."

In September 1851, three especially desperate fugitives came to his house. Their leader was William Parker of Pennsylvania, a free black who had hidden two runaway slaves. When their slaveholder, a man named Edward Gorsuch, and his son and police officers came after them, Parker and his friends, armed with sticks and guns, had attacked. Gorsuch had been killed and his son injured. Parker and the two runaways escaped. They traveled by way of

Runaway slaves and agents on the Underground Railroad circa 1800

the Underground Railroad to Rochester, where Douglass got them boat passage to Canada. "I returned to my house," Douglass later remembered, "with a sense of relief which I cannot stop here to describe."

Douglass wrote that he didn't think of Parker and the two runaways as killers. "To me they were heroic defenders of the just rights of men against men-stealers and murderers."

On the national stage, the relative calm following the Compromise of 1850 ended in 1854. People were eager to settle the large area of land west of Iowa and Missouri—the Kansas and Nebraska territories. Railroads wanted to lay track in these open territories and cross the continent, all the way to the Pacific Ocean. But would this land be slave or free? According to the Missouri Compromise of 1820, there would be no new slave territories north of Missouri's southern border. That meant this land would be free. But representatives of slave states objected, so a new compromise was brokered, the Kansas-Nebraska Act of 1854. It declared the citizens who lived there could decide whether to be slave or free.

On October 30, 1854, Douglass spoke about the Kansas-Nebraska Act before an audience of more than fifteen hundred people in Chicago. "This bill, this Nebraska bill," he said, "gives to the people of the territories the right to hold slaves. Where did this bill get this right, which it so generously gives away?"

The act led to unrest. In the Kansas territory, after a fraudulent election in which there were many more votes than voters, a proslavery legislature was appointed. "Free Soilers" objected and formed their own government. This led to violence, in both the territories and in Congress.

In Kansas, printing presses were destroyed; houses were looted and burned; people were tortured and killed. In the United States Senate, on May 19, 1856, antislavery senator Charles Sumner of Massachusetts began a two-day-long, strongly worded speech on the crimes in Kansas. This angered representatives of slave states and on May 21, Congressman Preston Brooks of South Carolina

Charles Sumner

charged Sumner and beat his head so viciously with a cane that it took Sumner three years to recover.

What was the reaction to the beating? Douglass wrote that "Southern ladies even applauded the armed bully for his murderous assault upon an unarmed Northern senator." To him, all this "foreshadowed a conflict on a larger scale."

In 1857, the Supreme Court struck another blow against abolition. Dred Scott, the slave of an army surgeon, claimed that since he had worked for several years in states and territories where slavery was unlawful, he should be set free. The court ruled against him: First, it ruled that as an African American born into slavery, he could not be a citizen and therefore had no right to sue in federal court; second, that Congress had no right to outlaw slavery in the territories.

"We are now told," Douglass said in an 1857 speech about the ruling, "that the day is lost—all lost—and that we may as well give up the struggle . . . that slaves are property in the same sense that horses, sheep, and swine are property. . . . Such a decision cannot stand."

Douglass's friend John Brown was determined not to give up the struggle. In 1855, Brown moved to Kansas, where, according to Douglass, he "met persecution with persecution, war with war, strategy with strategy, assassination and house-burning with signal and terrible retaliation. . . . The horrors wrought by his iron hand cannot be contemplated without a shudder, but it is the shudder which one feels at the execution of a murderer."

In May 1856, in what became known as the Pottawatomie Massacre, Brown and his followers pulled proslavery men from their cabins. Brown shot one man in the head, and others were brutally chopped to death. Douglass condemned the killings, but he said they were "the logical result of slave-holding persecutions."

In early 1858, Brown stayed in the Douglass home in Rochester for several weeks. He spent much of his time in his room working in private on plans for

John Brown in 1855 (l) and 1859 (r)

his next attack. In July 1859, he used the assumed name John Smith and rented a Maryland farmhouse just across the river from Harpers Ferry, Virginia.

The next month, Brown wrote to Douglass that he would soon begin "his work" and asked that they meet. Douglass went to a barbershop in Chambersburg, Pennsylvania, and from there was led to an old stone quarry. Brown, disguised as a fisherman, asked his friend to join an attack on a federal arsenal. It would be the beginning of what Brown hoped would be a slave revolt.

"Our talk was long and earnest," Douglass later wrote. "Brown for Harper's Ferry, and I against it; he for striking a blow which should instantly rouse the country, and I for the policy of gradually and uncountably drawing off the slaves to the mountains, as at first suggested and proposed by him."

When Douglass was about to leave, Brown hugged him and said, "Come with me, Douglass, I will defend you with my life. I want you for a special purpose. When I strike, the bees will begin to swarm, and I shall need you to help hive them."

The bees Brown spoke of were the slaves. He wanted Douglass to rally them, to convince them to join his revolution.

Douglass questioned whether it was discretion or cowardice that kept him from joining Brown. Whatever the reason, he returned home to Rochester.

John Brown commissioned himself a major general, and on Sunday night, October 16, 1859, he led an attack of more than twenty men on the United States armory at Harpers Ferry. They put out the town's streetlights, cut its telegraph wires, and captured a huge supply of rifles and ammunition. Along the way, they freed slaves and took hostages.

Harpers Ferry

When local militia came out and fought, Brown and his men took cover in a firehouse. They barricaded themselves into the building along with hostages. Brown continued to lead the uprising. With one son dead, Brown held another dying son in one arm while he held up a rifle in the other and shouted orders to his men. Early on Tuesday, ninety marines led by Colonel Robert E. Lee stormed the building. Ten of Brown's men were killed. Five escaped. John Brown was captured.

He was asked, "Are you Captain Brown?" He answered, "I am sometimes called so." He was asked what his intentions were, and he answered, "To free the slaves from bondage." Brown told Governor Henry Wise of Virginia that he had enough rifles, revolvers, spears, and tomahawks to arm 1,500 men. "I only regret I have failed in my designs."

Within two weeks of his capture, John Brown was tried and convicted of treason, conspiracy, and murder. He was sentenced to death by hanging. He had with him letters indicating that several people knew of his plans. "Gerrit Smith, Joshua Giddings, Fred Douglass and Other Abolitionist and Republicans Implicated" was the headline in a prominent New York newspaper. Douglass knew he was in trouble, that he might be arrested. He quickly fled to Canada.

On October 31, Douglass wrote a letter calling Brown a hero "whose one right hand has shaken the foundation of the American Union, and whose ghost will haunt the bed-chambers of all the born and unborn slaveholders of Virginia." And to those who questioned why he did not join in the revolt, Douglass answered, "Let every man work for the abolition of Slavery in his own way."

On November 12, Douglass sailed from Canada to England, a trip he had planned before the ill-fated Harpers Ferry raid.

Not everyone saw John Brown as a hero. While he was in prison, he received a letter from Matilda Doyle, whose husband and two sons Brown had killed a few years earlier in the Pottawatomie Massacre.

"Although vengeance is not mine," she wrote, "I confess I do feel gratified to hear that you were stopped in your fiendish career at Harper's Ferry with the loss of your two sons. You can now appreciate my distress in Kansas, when you then and there entered my house at midnight, and arrested my husband and two boys, and took them to the yard, and in cold blood shot them dead in my bearing. You can't say you done it to free our slaves; we had none, and never expected to have. . . . While I feel for your folly, I hope and trust you will meet your just reward." In a postscript, Doyle wrote that her son John, whose life was spared at Pottawatomie, wanted to be at Brown's execution, "that he might adjust the rope around your neck."

Money was collected to send John Doyle to the hanging, but when the family realized he could not get there in time, the trip was canceled.

On Friday morning, December 2, John Brown was taken from prison in an open wagon along with the pine box that would be his coffin. He was heavily guarded as he was transported to a large wheat field. Brown was calm as he approached the gallows. "You are a game man," someone said to him. "Yes," he replied. "I was so trained; it was one of the lessons of my mother."

Brown's arms were tied. His head was placed in the noose, the boards beneath his feet were pulled away, and after a few slight struggles he was dead.

At the time of Brown's execution, Douglass was in England. People there went to his lectures. They were eager to hear him talk about slavery, John Brown, and Harpers Ferry.

After about six months in England, Douglass hoped to cross the English Channel and visit France. For that he needed a special visa. He applied to the American consulate. His request was denied because he was an African American—as ruled in the Dred Scott decision, he was not a citizen. He applied directly to France and was quickly given the necessary papers.

But tragic news forced him to cancel his plans to cross the Channel. His beloved youngest child, his ten-year-old daughter, Annie, had died. He took the first steamship home.

Chapter Eleven

"TO ARMS!"

No state upon its own mere motion
can lawfully get out of the Union.
—ABRAHAM LINCOLN, IN HIS FIRST
INAUGURAL ADDRESS, 1861

BY MID-1860, the Harpers Ferry confrontation was history. John Brown was already an abolitionist martyr. "John Brown's Song," soon lto be a Union Army marching song, was wildly popular in the Northern states. Wary of creating more martyrs for the cause, federal officers were not pursuing Brown's alleged accomplices. So in May 1860, there was little chance of being arrested, and Frederick Douglass returned to Rochester.

The country had other issues now. It was in the midst of the presidential election campaign of 1860.

The Democratic Party had split. The Southern faction nominated John C. Breckenridge of Kentucky for president, and the Northern faction nominated Stephen A. Douglas of Illinois. The Constitutional Union Party, which was formed when the Whig and Know-Nothing parties merged, nominated John Bell of Tennessee.

John Brown's Song

John Brown's body lies a-mouldering in the grave,
John Brown's body lies a-mouldering in the grave,
John Brown's body lies a-mouldering in the grave,
His soul goes marching on.

Chorus
Glory, glory, hallelujah, Glory, glory, hallelujah,
Glory, glory, hallelujah, His soul goes marching on.

He's gone to be a soldier in the Army of the Lord,
He's gone to be a soldier in the Army of the Lord,
He's gone to be a soldier in the Army of the Lord,
His soul goes marching on.

Chorus

John Brown's knapsack is strapped upon his back,
John Brown's knapsack is strapped upon his back,
John Brown's knapsack is strapped upon his back,
His soul goes marching on.

Chorus

John Brown died that the slaves might be free,
John Brown died that the slaves might be free,
John Brown died that the slaves might be free,
His soul goes marching on.

Chorus

The stars above in Heaven now are looking kindly down,
The stars above in Heaven now are looking kindly down,
The stars above in Heaven now are looking kindly down,
His soul goes marching on.

Chorus

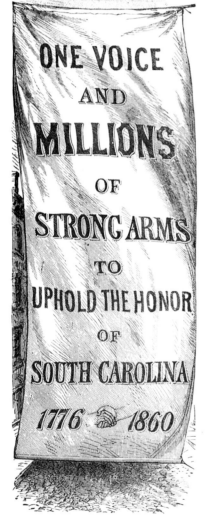

A street banner in Charleston, South Carolina, calling for volunteers to join the Confederate Army

The recently founded Republican Party nominated Abraham Lincoln of Illinois. And Frederick Douglass's friend Gerrit Smith was the candidate of the Radical Abolitionist Party.

The big issue of the campaign was slavery in the territories. Breckenridge said he would allow it. Douglas stood for territorial sovereignty, which meant he was in favor of allowing the citizens of each territory to decide whether to be slave or free. Bell tried to avoid the issue by vaguely declaring for "the Constitution of the country, the union of the states, and the enforcement of the laws." Lincoln and the Republicans pledged to tolerate slavery where it existed but not allow it beyond the fifteen slave states. Smith pledged to abolish it completely.

Smith, who was the cousin of women's rights advocate Elizabeth Cady Stanton, was wealthy and generous. He gave land and money to thousands of African Americans and had helped finance John Brown's attack on Harpers Ferry. At first, Frederick Douglass supported his candidacy. But realizing that Smith had no hope of winning, he shifted his support to Lincoln.

"Into this contest I threw myself," Douglass later wrote. In the June 1860 issue of his now monthly newspaper, he declared that Lincoln was "a man of unblemished private character" with "great firmness of will."

The campaign bitterly divided the country. In October, Governor William Henry Gist of South Carolina and other prominent state politicians resolved that if Lincoln was elected, the state would leave the Union. Gist sent messages to other Southern governors declaring that South Carolina would secede alone or with whichever states would join them.

The election was held on November 6.

Lincoln lost in all the slave states but won all the electors of every free state except New Jersey, which was split between him and Douglas. Lincoln had less than 40 percent of the popular vote, but he won 180 electors, more than all the other candidates combined. His inauguration was set for March 4, 1861.

On December 20, 1860, the South Carolina legislature met and formally declared the state was no longer part of the United States. When the news got out, large banners and signs announcing THE UNION IS DISSOLVED! were posted. To celebrate, people rang bells and fired cannons. Women wore cotton secession bonnets with palm decorations, a tribute to South Carolina, nicknamed the Palmetto State.

By the beginning of February, six other states—Mississippi, Florida, Alabama, Georgia, Louisiana, and Texas—had voted to join South Carolina. On February 4, representatives from six of those states met in Montgomery, Alabama, and formed the Confederate States of America. They chose Jefferson Davis of Mississippi and Alexander H. Stephens of Georgia as their president and vice president. They made Richmond, Virginia, their capital.

A Confederate constitution was written and ratified. Davis formed a government and appointed a cabinet, with secretaries of state, war, navy, treasury, and post office. He called for 100,000 volunteers for the Confederate army.

"Still we doubted if anything serious would come of it," Douglass later wrote. "We treated it as a bubble on the wave."

Jefferson Davis

The states in rebellion seized customhouses, arsenals, forts, and navy yards within their borders. President James Buchanan didn't challenge these takeovers, seeming to agree that a state legislature had the right to do what it wanted within its borders. By the time Lincoln was inaugurated, only a few Southern military posts, including Fort Pickens in Florida and Fort Sumter in South Carolina, remained in federal control.

On April 12, there were just seventy soldiers inside Fort Sumter. There were seven thousand Confederate troops outside the fort when, at four thirty in the morning, Confederates fired on it. By the next day, the heavy bombardment had set it on fire. Federal troops, exhausted and almost blinded by the smoke, surrendered. Amazingly, even with all the gunfire from both sides, no one was killed. But on April 14, at a planned hundred-gun salute honoring the American flag before it was lowered, a gun exploded, killing Private Daniel Hough of the United States Army, was the first soldier to die in the Civil War.

President James Buchanan

The firing on Fort Sumter, South Carolina

"To arms!" people in the Northern states called out. "The Union must be preserved!"

In the free states, people wore Union badges and displayed flags. In New York City, there was a mass meeting

calling for war. Even Stephen A. Douglas, who had been somewhat conciliatory to the South in the presidential campaign, changed his stance. "There can be no neutrals now," he said, "only patriots and traitors."

"For the moment," Frederick Douglass later wrote, "the Northern lamb was transformed into a lion, and his roar was terrible. But he only showed his teeth, and clearly had no wish to use them."

On April 15, just after the surrender of Fort Sumter, Lincoln called for seventy-five thousand volunteer troops. The nation was at war with itself, one section against another.

There was a great response to Lincoln's call. By July 1861, there were more than 180,000 soldiers in the Union army. In contrast, there were some 110,000 soldiers in the Confederate army. By 1863, the disparity in the two armies was even greater; by then, there were almost 700,000 in the Union army and about 300,000 Confederates.

On April 19, eight hundred new Union troops, the Sixth Massachusetts Regiment, were on a train headed south to Washington, D.C. When the train reached Baltimore, it was met by a wild mob carrying a secessionist flag. Windows were smashed with stones and bricks. Sand, stones, and large metal objects were thrown on the tracks. Union soldiers fired their guns. By the time the Baltimore police restored order, four soldiers and twelve civilians had been killed.

By June 1861, Virginia, Arkansas, North Carolina, and Tennessee had voted to secede, making a total of eleven Confederate states. Four slave states bordering the north—Missouri, Kentucky, Delaware, and Maryland—didn't join. West Virginia separated from Virginia and became a new state that remained a part of the Union.

People in the North were eager to end the rebellion with one mighty show of force. On Sunday, July 21, 1861, with cries of "On to Richmond!" a Union force of about thirty-five thousand soldiers advanced on an almost equal number of Confederates at a bridge over Bull Run, a stream near Manassas Junction, Virginia, just twenty-five miles southwest of Washington, D.C.

Members of Congress and sightseers carrying picnic baskets came from the capital to watch. The battlefield was soon hidden by smoke from all the gunfire, and it wasn't until several hours later that they saw Union troops retreat in panic to Washington.

A total of almost five thousand Union and Confederate soldiers were killed or injured at Bull Run. The casualties shocked the nation.

From the beginning, the Union army's aims were to take Richmond, split the Confederacy by taking control of the forts along the Mississippi River, and block Southern harbors. The Confederates hoped only to rid their land of the enemy.

What was the source of the conflict? "Since his inauguration," the *New York Herald* wrote of President Lincoln in December 1861, "he has declared that, in the prosecution of this war, he looks to integrity of the Union—nothing less, but nothing more."

Douglass disagreed. "From the first," he later wrote, "I, for one, saw in this war the end of slavery." All the talk of the war being about anything other than slavery was nonsense, he told a New York audience of two thousand in July 1862. He continued, "The only choice left to this nation is abolition or destruction. You must abolish slavery, or abandon the Union."

Douglass saw African Americans as the key to a Union victory. He questioned why the North didn't recruit blacks, why it fought "with their soft white hand while they kept their black iron hand chained and helpless behind them."

In the South, slaves served the Confederacy in fields, factories, and homes, leaving Southern men free to fight. Freeing the slaves, Douglass said, would cripple the rebellion.

By the middle of 1862, it seemed Lincoln and Congress had heard him.

On July 17, Congress passed legislation allowing the enlistment of blacks into the Union army. On September 22, 1862, just days after the Battle of Antietam, in which more than 23,500 men were killed or wounded, President Lincoln signed the Emancipation Proclamation, declaring that as of January 1, 1863, all slaves in the Confederacy would be free. With that proclamation, the Civil War became a fight both to save the Union and to free the slaves.

in due time ~~at the next session of Congress~~

And the executive will recommend that

all citizens of the United States who shall have remained loyal thereto throughout the rebellion, shall (upon the restoration of the constitutional relation between the United States, and their respective states, and people, if that relation shall have been suspended or disturbed) be compensated for all losses by acts of the United States, including the loss of slaves.

In witness whereof, I have

L. S.   hereunto set my hand, and caused the seal of the United States to be affixed

Done at the City of Washington, this twenty second day of September, in the year of our Lord, one thousand, eight hundred and sixty two, and sixty two, and of the Independence of the United States, the eighty seventh.

Abraham Lincoln

By the President.
William H Seward,
Secretary of State

Chapter Twelve

"A SACRED EFFORT"

All persons held as slaves within any State,
the people whereof shall then be in rebellion
against the United States, shall be then,
thenceforward, and forever free.

—From the Emancipation
Proclamation, effective January 1, 1863

On New Year's Day 1863, Frederick Douglass was in Boston. He and more than three thousand others, mostly African Americans, had crowded into Tremont Temple, a Baptist church sometimes used for public events. They were excited, anxiously waiting news from Washington. Close to midnight, someone rushed from the telegraph office with a message. The long-awaited Emancipation Proclamation had become law.

People threw their hats in the air. They shouted for joy. "God Almighty's New Year," a minister proclaimed, "will make the United States the land of freedom!" Then Douglass led the crowd in singing a hymn.

Lincoln's proclamation declared that only slaves in the Confederacy would be free. At the time, it didn't bring real freedom to many slaves—just the few hundred in Southern battle zones controlled by the Union army. The editors of the *New York Herald* even declared Lincoln's proclamation to be "practically

Facing page: A page from the draft of Lincoln's preliminary Emancipation Proclamation

a dead letter." But it wasn't. Despite its limitations, it told leaders of the rebellion that there was no going back. Defeat or surrender meant the end of slavery in the Confederate states. When some slaves heard of the proclamation, they quickly escaped to freedom behind Union army lines.

Looking to the future, Douglass asked, "What shall be done with the four million slaves, if they are emancipated?" His answer: "Do nothing with them; mind your business and let them mind theirs. . . . If you see him ploughing in the open field, leveling the forest, at work with 'a spade, a rake, a hoe, a pickaxe, or a bill,' let him alone: he has a right to work. If you see him on the way to school, with spelling-book, geography, and arithmetic in his hands, let him alone. Don't shut the door in his face, or bolt your gates against him; he has a right to learn; let him alone. Don't pass laws to degrade him."

Tennessee was already under Union control, so the Proclamation did not free its slaves. Tennessee's milatary governor was Andrew Johnson, soon to be Lincoln's vice president.

Excerpt from the *New York Herald,* January 3, 1863

The **confirmatory emancipation** proclamation of President Lincoln is before our readers. It declares "all the slave population now, hence forward forever free" in the following named States and parts of States, to wit: Number of Slaves.

The States and parts of States recognizing slavery exempted from the proclamation, or in which the slaves are to remain slaves, are:— States: Number of Slaves.

States	Number of Slaves
Arkansas	111,104
Alabama	435,132
Florida	61,753
Georgia	462,232
Mississippi	436,696
North Carolina	331,081
South Carolina	402,541
Texas	180,682
Virginia (part held by rebels)	450,437
Louisiana (parishes held by rebels)	247,734
Total slaves declared free	**3,119,392**

States	Number of Slaves
Delaware	1,798
Kentucky	225,490
Maryland	87,188
Missouri	114,465
Tennessee	275,784
Louisiana (parishes re-conquered)	85,281
West Virginia and eastern counties recovered	41,000
Total slaves excluded from freedom	**831,006**

Also in the proclamation was the statement that African American volunteers "of suitable condition" would be accepted into the armed services of the United States. Douglass rallied them. "Men of Color to Arms," he wrote in his monthly newspaper. "Liberty won by white men would lose half its lustre." Among the very first African American recruits in the Union army were his sons Lewis Henry and Charles Remond. Later, Frederick Jr. also signed up.

On May 28, 1863, drummer boys led a column of black soldiers through the streets of Boston. It was the 54th Massachusetts Regiment. Sergeant Major Lewis Henry Douglass was among them. Frederick Douglass stood on the dock and watched his son's regiment board a ship and then leave the harbor.

On July 18, after marching day and night, in wind and rain, the regiment led an assault on heavily fortified Fort Wagner, South Carolina. They charged through gunfire and engaged the enemy in hand-to-hand combat. At last, they were driven back. Casualties were high, but just one indication of the valor of the men was Flag Sergeant Corney, bloodied and exhausted, who staggered back with his men and proudly announced, "The old flag never touched the ground!" The heroism of this black regiment encouraged more African Americans to enlist.

Douglass had assured African American recruits that they would be treated as the equals of white soldiers, but they weren't. They were paid less than whites and given less training and inferior weapons. They could not easily become officers. When they were captured by the Confederates, they were often sold into slavery or shot. Douglass wrote in his autobiography, "The attitude of the government at Washington caused me deep sadness and discouragement."

On August 10, Douglass took his complaints to President Lincoln.

"I shall never forget my first interview with this great man," he later wrote. "Happily for me there was no vain pomp and ceremony about him. I was never more quickly or more completely put at ease in the presence of a great man, than in that of Abraham Lincoln. . . . The room bore the marks of business, and the persons in it, the president included, appeared to be much overworked and tired."

Douglass told Lincoln of the unfair treatment of black soldiers, and Lincoln replied that having blacks in uniform was already a great step forward, that just a few years before, it could not have happened. He also promised there would be further progress.

Douglass went next to meet with Secretary of War Edwin Stanton. When he related his discussion with President Lincoln, Stanton said that "justice would ultimately be done."

Stanton offered to make Douglass an officer, an assistant to General Lorenzo Thomas, who was recruiting and organizing troops in the Mississippi valley. Douglass accepted, but after he left Stanton's office, he heard no more about the commission. He thought later that the government had wanted to keep its "positions of honor" for white men, that it was not ready for a "policy of perfect equality."

Some 180,000 African Americans, both freemen and runaway slaves, served in the Union army and navy. Seventeen were awarded the Congressional Medal for valor. Colonel Beard of the 48th New York Infantry wrote in a report that black soldiers "fought with astonishing coolness and bravery. I found them all I could desire. They behaved gloriously, and deserve all praise."

Surprisingly, the Confederacy enlisted blacks before the Union did. According to Union Sergeant Major Christian Fleetwood, an African American Congressional Medal of Honor winner, "There is no telling what the result of the war might have been had the South kept up the policy of enlisting the freemen and emancipating the slaves and their families. . . . The early successes of the South closed its eyes to its only chances."

About the time black soldiers were first enlisting into the Union army, the first Conscription Act was passed. While it drafted men between eighteen and thirty-five years of age into service, it also allowed them to pay others to serve in their places. In July 1863, to the cries of "Rich man's war, poor man's fight," there were three days of riots in New York City.

An 1863 letter declaring Douglass to be a free man

Mixed in with the anger over the draft was antiblack sentiment. People claimed they were willing to fight to preserve the Union but not to free the slaves.

According to Douglass, the rioters were joined by "thieves, burglars, pickpockets, incendiaries and jailbirds." There was looting. Fires were set. Blacks were dragged from their homes, and more than a hundred were killed. Douglass went to New York during the riots and was horrified when he heard that Governor Horatio Seymour addressed the ruffians who were terrorizing the city as "my friends." Had he been true to the Union, Douglass felt, "he would have burned his tongue with a red hot iron sooner than allow it to call these thugs, thieves, and murderers his 'friends.'"

On the battlefield in July 1863, General Ulysses S. Grant's Union troops took Vicksburg, Mississippi, an important garrison along the Mississippi River, splitting Southern forces. In November, Grant took Chattanooga, Tennessee, and opened the way for an invasion of Georgia.

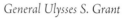

General Ulysses S. Grant

In April 1864, Grant was given command of the entire Union army. Douglass was pleased. He wrote, "There was a moral as well as military basis" for his faith in Grant, who "had shown his single-mindedness and superiority to popular prejudice by his prompt cooperation with President Lincoln in his policy of employing colored troops, and his order commanding his soldiers to treat such troops with due respect."

In August 1864, with Grant leading his troops toward Richmond, Virginia, Lincoln asked Douglass to meet with him again. "What he said on this day," Douglass later wrote, "showed a deeper moral conviction against slavery than I had ever seen before in anything spoken or written by him." Lincoln said that despite his proclamation, few slaves had left their masters. Douglass replied that surely few were aware of the proclamation, because slaveholders knew how to keep such things from their slaves. At Lincoln's suggestion, Douglass agreed to organize African American scouts to go into Confederate areas and tell slaves of the Emancipation Proclamation. But the war ended before Douglass could recruit volunteers to serve on this dangerous mission.

Shortly after his meeting with Lincoln, Douglass returned to Baltimore. It had been twenty-six years since he escaped the city and slavery. Douglass gave lectures and was reunited with his sister Eliza, who had bought her freedom and that of her nine children.

The Republicans renominated Lincoln in 1864. His running mate was a Democrat, Andrew Johnson of Tennessee. But the Republican Party was split. The radical Republicans called for an immediate end to slavery and a harsher treatment of the rebellious states. Their candidate was John C. Fremont of California.

The Democrats denounced Lincoln. They called his presidency "years of failure to restore the Union by the experiment of war." They promised to make peace, even if it meant two separate nations. Their candidate was George B. McClellan of New Jersey, a former commander of the Union army. McClellan repudiated his party's peace platform but accepted its nomination. "I could not look in the faces of my gallant comrades," he said, "and tell them that their labors and the sacrifice of so many of our slain and wounded brethren had been in vain."

Lincoln was reelected by a huge majority.

Douglass was at Lincoln's inauguration. He later wrote, "There was a leaden stillness about the crowd." He also wrote, "I made a discovery in regard to the vice president—Andrew Johnson. . . . Mr. Lincoln touched Mr. Johnson, and pointed me out to him. The first expression which came to his face, and which I think was the true index of his heart, was one of bitter contempt and aversion. Seeing that I observed him, he tried to assume a more friendly appearance; but it was too late." Douglass turned and said to the African American woman standing beside him, "Whatever Andrew Johnson may be, he certainly is no friend of our race."

In his first inaugural address, Lincoln had said, "I have no purpose, directly or indirectly, to interfere with the institution of slavery in the States where it exists." That disappointed Douglass. Now he wondered, with the war almost won, what the president would say.

The morning of March 4, 1865, was rainy, but as Lincoln stepped forward and started to speak, the sun came out. "It became clear as it could be," an observer wrote in his diary, "and calm."

The president's speech was brief, just over seven hundred words. "Fondly do we hope, fervently do we pray—that this mighty scourge of war may speedily pass away." He wondered if perhaps God willed the war to continue until "every drop of blood drawn with the lash, shall be paid by another drawn with the sword. . . . let us strive on to finish the work we are in; to bind up the nation's wounds . . . to do all which may achieve and cherish a just and lasting peace among ourselves and with all nations."

That night, Douglass went to congratulate the president on his fine speech. But two policemen at the door of the White House told him to leave, saying that no African Americans were to go in. "I told the officers I was quite sure there must be some mistake," Douglass later wrote, "for no such order could have emanated from President Lincoln; and if he knew I was at the door he would desire my admission." The officers then politely offered to take Douglass

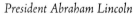

President Abraham Lincoln

General Robert E. Lee

Union soldiers sharing their rations with Confederates after the Army of Northern Virginia surrenders at Appomattox Court House, Virginia

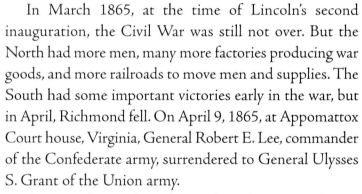

in, but instead they led him to an exit. "You deceived me," Douglass said. "I shall not go out of this building till I see President Lincoln." Just then, someone recognized him. Douglass asked the man to please tell the president that he was outside.

At last, Douglass entered the East Room of the White House. Lincoln saw him and said, "Here comes my friend Douglass." The president took his hand and said, "I am glad to see you. I saw you in the crowd today, listening to my inaugural address; how did you like it? . . . There is no man in the country whose opinion I value more than yours." Douglass told President Lincoln he liked the speech, that it was "a sacred effort."

Douglass found out later that the two police officers had no orders to keep blacks out, that they were just "complying with an old custom, the outgrowth of slavery." Douglass felt the best way to break down such practices was simply to confront them.

In March 1865, at the time of Lincoln's second inauguration, the Civil War was still not over. But the North had more men, many more factories producing war goods, and more railroads to move men and supplies. The South had some important victories early in the war, but in April, Richmond fell. On April 9, 1865, at Appomattox Court house, Virginia, General Robert E. Lee, commander of the Confederate army, surrendered to General Ulysses S. Grant of the Union army.

On April 14, five days after the surrender at Appomattox, Lincoln went with his wife to Ford's Theatre in Washington, D.C., to see a performance of a comedy, *Our American Cousin*. He sat in a rocking chair in a box overlooking the stage. At about 10:15 p.m., John Wilkes Booth, an actor and crazed supporter of slavery, the Confederacy, and secession, entered the president's box. He took a few steps toward Lincoln's chair and shot the president in the head. Many of the people in the theater were absorbed in the action on the stage and didn't hear the shot. Booth dropped his gun, waved a hunting knife at the others in the box, and then

Ford's Theatre, where Lincoln was shot

jumped to the stage. He shouted, *"Sic semper tyrannis!"* (Thus always to tyrants!), rushed out the back door, got on his horse and rode off.

By the next morning, President Lincoln was dead.

Booth escaped, first to Maryland, then to Virginia. Thousands of police officers and soldiers chased after him, and on April 26 they found him hiding in a barn. He refused to surrender, and the barn was set on fire. Booth picked up a gun, and a soldier shot him from behind. Five hours later he was dead. Booth wasn't alone in the plot to kill the president. In July, four conspirators were hanged, four others were given prison sentences.

Frederick Douglass was in Rochester when he heard of the Lincoln assassination. He was terribly shaken by the news. He described Lincoln as a *"great man—too great to be small in anything. In his company I was never in any way reminded of my humble origin, or of my unpopular color."* And if he needed any proof of the closeness the president held for him, it came from Lincoln's widow, who gave Douglass her slain husband's ivory-handled walking stick.

A reward poster for seeking the capture of Booth

The house in which Lincoln died

When people in Rochester received news of Lincoln's death, they gathered at the city hall. "I was called upon," Douglass remembered many years later, "and spoke out of the fullness of my heart, and, happily, I gave expression to so much of the soul of the people present. . . . We shared in common a terrible calamity, and this 'touch of nature,' made us more than countrymen, it made us 'kin.' "

"This is not an occasion for speech making," Douglass said, "but for silence." He spoke of the last time he had been with the president, when "I shook his brave, honest hand, and looked into his gentle eye."

Later, someone who heard Douglass speak that day said, "I never heard truer eloquence! I never saw profounder impression. When he was finished, the meeting was done."

Chapter Thirteen

"YOUNG IN LIBERTY AND OLD IN SLAVERY"

I never before saw children so eager to learn.
—Charlotte Forten,
an African American who went to
South Carolina in the early 1860s
to teach black children

With the end of the Civil War, "a strange and, perhaps, perverse feeling" came over Douglass. His joy over the end of slavery "was slightly tinged with a feeling of sadness." He felt he "had reached the end of the noblest and best part" of his life, that his greatest work was done, that his "voice was no longer needed."

"Where shall I go?" he wondered. What should he do now?

Douglass wrote later that he soon realized "the wrongs to my people were not ended."

On December 18, 1865, the Thirteenth Amendment, which abolished slavery in every part of the nation, was officially added to the Constitution. Slaves had gained their freedom but little else. They had no jobs, no money, no homes, and no property. In many places, their rights were restricted. At speaking engagements at colleges and literary societies, Douglass referred to these many injustices. He felt he was "in some small measure helping" to lift his people.

He had a clear vision of what equality meant. In 1865, the Educational Monument Association was formed to build a college for blacks as a memorial to Lincoln. Douglass was asked to join the association. He refused. He wrote in a letter that he disapproved of "building up permanent separate institutions for colored people." Perhaps the brilliant Douglass could sense the damage the doctrine of "separate but equal" would cause.

At the 1865 annual meeting of the Anti-Slavery Society, William Lloyd Garrison proposed that since slavery was abolished, "never, never to be reversed," the society should end its work. Douglass disagreed. He spoke of the need "not merely to emancipate, but to elevate the enslaved class."

Most African Americans lived in Southern states, in areas devastated by four years of almost constant fighting. By 1865, all that was left of many fine Southern homes were piles of stones and blackened chimneys. Store shelves were empty. Schools and churches were closed. Teachers and their students, ministers and their congregants, had scattered. Barns had been leveled. Fences and the animals they had corralled—horses, cows, and hogs—were gone. Railroad tracks had been torn up. Steamboats had been sunk. Riverways were blocked, wharves and docks destroyed, and the money that people in the South had worked for and saved, Confederate money, was worthless.

Southern families were broken, too. Soldiers returned to wives and children they hadn't seen in months, sometimes years. Many came home on crutches. Many more never came home.

The broken South had few plans to help newly freed slaves.

Soldiers returning home after the war

Lincoln had promised to restore the nation "with charity for all." But he was gone, and the new president, Andrew Johnson, was a shaky leader with little support in Congress. Restrictive "black codes," which many whites in the South claimed were needed to help restore order, became the law in many places. These codes kept blacks from owning guns or whiskey, from going outside at night, testifying in court, and meeting in groups. The codes made it difficult for blacks to rent or lease farmland.

President Andrew Johnson

"From the first," Douglass later wrote, he saw "no chance of bettering the condition of the freedman, until he should cease to be merely a freedman and should become a citizen." The right to vote "was essential to the freedom of the freedman."

There was great resistance, both in the South and in the North, to allowing blacks to vote. The principal argument against African American suffrage was that they just were not ready for it. To that claim Douglass said, "As one learns to swim by swimming, the Negro must learn how to vote by voting."

On February 7, 1866, a delegation of African Americans, including Douglass and his son Lewis Henry, met with President Johnson to ask him to support black suffrage. George T. Downing of Rhode Island spoke first. He said the group had come to the White House as "friends meeting a friend." Then Douglass told the president, "[T]he fact that we are the subjects of the Government," that blacks pay taxes and are drafted to serve in the army, "makes it not improper that we should ask to share in the privileges of this condition."

Johnson wasn't swayed. He said he was willing to lead African Americans "from bondage to freedom" but not to support black suffrage, which, he claimed, would cause "great injury to the white as well as to the colored man." He talked for some forty-five minutes. When he was done, he refused to discuss the matter further. Downing and others in the delegation were sure Johnson's ideas would be "paraded before the country in the morning papers," so that night they asked Douglass to write a response.

"Peace between races is not to be secured by degrading one race and exalting another," Douglass wrote in a letter addressed to the president that was published in the *Washington Chroncile*, "but by maintaining a state of equal justice between all classes."

Soon after the meeting with Johnson, Congress passed the Civil Rights Act. It declared African Americans to be citizens entitled to the same privileges as whites. Two years later, the Fourteenth Amendment was added to the Constitution. It prohibited the laws of any states to take away the rights of any citizen without "due process of law."

In September 1866, an almost exclusively white convention in support of the rights of African Americans was held in Philadelphia. Douglass was elected to represent his hometown of Rochester, but a committee asked him not to attend. They said that having him there might cause trouble. Douglass saw real irony in their request. They wanted to discuss the principles of black rights without practicing them. "You might as well ask me to put a loaded pistol to my head," he wrote the committee, "as to ask me to keep out of this convention."

On September 3, the delegates gathered at Philadelphia's Independence Hall to walk by twos to National Hall, where they would have their meeting. Douglass was the only African American in the group, and it seemed he would have to walk alone. But then Theodore Tilton, a poet and editor from New York, took his arm and walked with him. Douglass later wrote, "I think I never appreciated an act of courage and generous sentiment more highly than I did of this brave young man."

They walked together, and the people of Philadelphia cheered for Douglass. Then, on the corner of Ninth and Chestnut Streets, he met Mrs. Amanda Sears, the daughter of Lucretia Auld. She lived in Baltimore. "I heard you were to be here," she said, "and I came to see you walk in this procession."

They had met once, seven years earlier. In 1859, just after Douglass lectured in National Hall, he received a note that Amanda Sears had been in the audience and that her husband had an office nearby. Douglass went to the office and met John Sears, who complained about the book *Narrative of the Life of Frederick Douglass*. Sears said what was written about his father-in-law, Thomas

Auld, was not true, that he was a good man and a kind master. They talked awhile, and at last Douglass asked if he could meet Miss Amanda. "This request was a little too much for him at first," Douglass later wrote, "and he put me off by saying that she was a mere child when I last saw her, and she was now a mother of a large family of children, and I would not know her." Douglass disagreed. He said he "could select Miss Amanda out of a thousand other ladies."

At last, Sears relented. He invited Douglass to come to his home the next afternoon.

Douglass put on his best suit and hired the finest carriage available. He wanted to show Miss Amanda how far he had come since he had escaped slavery. John Sears made the reunion quite a party by inviting lots of his friends.

Douglass entered the parlor and realized he was being tested. Sears wanted him to make good on his boast, that he could pick Miss Amanda out from a large group of strangers. The last time he had seen her, she was a small, thin child. There, in the middle of the room, was a petite woman in a rocking chair with a little girl at her side. Douglass knew she was Miss Amanda. "If you will allow me," he said to his host, "I will select Miss Amanda from this company." As he started toward her, she rose and hurried to him. "All thought of slavery, color, or what might seem to belong to the dignity of her position vanished, and the meeting was as the meeting of friends long separated, yet still present in each other's memory and affection."

Amanda Sears lived in Maryland, a slave state. Though this was six years before the passage of the Thirteenth Amendment, she had freed all her slaves. She appreciated the many nice things Douglass had written about her mother, who had died when Amanda was very young.

Seeing Amanda Sears again, in 1866, reminded Douglass of how far he had come over the past almost thirty years, how far the nation had come. "Here was the daughter of the owner of a slave," he later wrote, "following with enthusiasm that slave as a free man, and listening with joy to the plaudits he received as he marched along through the crowded streets of the great city."

Almost twenty years later, when Amanda Sears was on her deathbed, she

Rosetta Douglass Sprague

Lewis H. Douglass

asked to see Douglass again, for him to tell her whatever he could about her mother, whom she expected to meet soon in "another and better world."

In 1867, Douglass had another emotional reunion, this time with his brother Perry, who had been a slave for more than fifty years. Perry Downs traveled with his wife and four children from Texas to New York to see his now-famous brother. In a letter, Douglass wrote that their meeting was "an event altogether too affecting to describe."

With the war over, the Douglass children—Rosetta, Lewis Henry, Frederick Jr., and Charles Remond—started families of their own. Rosetta married Nathan Sprague and in 1864 had a daughter, Anne, the first Douglass grandchild. She left the baby with Anna Douglass, the baby's grandmother, and worked in her father's office. She later became a teacher in New Jersey.

In 1869, Lewis married Helen Amelia Loguen, the daughter of a New York minister. He worked in Washington, D.C., first for the city legislature, then as a special agent of the post office, and then in real estate. In 1871, Frederick Jr. married Virginia L. Hewlett of Massachusetts. He worked in the courts of Washington, D.C. Charles Remond returned to Rochester and in 1866 married Mary Murphy. He worked in the War Department and the Treasury Department.

Many people, blacks and whites, encouraged Douglass to run for office, for either a seat in the House of Representatives or the Senate, but he declined. "I had small faith in my aptitude as a politician," he wrote, also saying, "I have never regretted that I did not enter the arena of congressional honors to which I was invited."

In May 1866, the American Equal Rights Association was formed to gain the vote for both blacks and women. Douglass was made one of the association's vice presidents, but he insisted it was more urgent for blacks to get the vote, even if it meant that women had to wait. That put him at odds with many of the association's leaders. When women "are objects of insult and outrage at every turn," he explained, "when they are in danger of having their homes burnt down over their heads; when their children are not allowed to enter schools; then they will have an urgency to obtain the ballot."

In 1870, the Fifteenth Amendment was ratified. It declared that the right of all citizens to vote shall not be denied "on account of race, color, or previous condition of servitude." At a celebration in Baltimore, the city in which he had worked as a slave, Douglass stated that now "everything is possible to us."

Also in 1870, Douglass became the editor of a weekly newspaper, *The New National Era*. He moved to Washington, D.C., to work on the paper, which was intended to be "an Advocate and an Educator" for newly freed slaves. "Free men, free soil, free speech, a free press, everywhere in the land" was its motto. "The ballot for all, education for all, fair wages for all." Douglass later called his work on the newspaper a "misadventure." He was proud of its content, but despite thousands of dollars of his own that he invested, he couldn't keep the paper going. It shut down in 1874.

Unfortunately for Douglass, this unsuccessful business was followed by another. On March 14, 1874, he was made president of the Freedman's Savings and Trust Company, a bank designed for hardworking African Americans, especially in the Southern states. The bank had a large, impressive main office in Washington, D.C., thirty-four branch offices from New Orleans to Philadelphia, and millions of dollars in assets. Douglass spent the first six weeks on the job checking the bank's financial condition. He found it to be "insolvent and irrecoverable" and concluded that he "was married to a corpse. The fine building was there with its marble counters and black walnut finishes, the affable and agile clerks, and the discreet and comely colored cashier; but the *life*, which was the money, was gone." By June 20, a little more than three months after he was named president, the bank closed. With the bank's failure, many African Americans lost their savings. Douglass himself lost thousands of dollars. The sad legacy of the Freedman's bank was that some blacks became reluctant to save or trust banks.

After these business reversals Douglass returned to the lecture circuit, where he was still very popular. He had many interests and among the topics of his talks were folklore, Scandinavian history, and self-made men.

During this time tragedy struck the Douglass family. On June 2, 1872, their Rochester home burned. Douglass's wife, Anna, and Rosetta and her family

Frederick Douglass Jr.

Charles Remond Douglass

were all in the house. They escaped, but books, letters, pictures, and furniture were lost. Fire was a favorite weapon of violent groups opposed to the advancement of African Americans, and the local fire company suspected that the fire had been deliberately set. Douglass's friends urged him to rebuild his home, but he didn't. Instead, the family moved to Washington.

Douglass lived in exciting times. And when change was afoot, somehow he seemed always to be in the middle of it.

Women couldn't vote in 1872, but they could hold elective office. For the first time, a woman was a candidate for president of the United States. At a convention in New York City's Apollo Hall, delegates to the Equal Rights Party nominated Victoria C. Woodhull. Douglass, who was not there, was nominated for vice president. He turned down the nomination and instead supported Ulysses S. Grant, who was reelected.

In 1876, Rutherford B. Hayes of Ohio was elected president, and in 1877 he named Douglass to the well-paying position of marshal of Washington, D.C. The appointment needed Senate approval, which was granted. Douglass became the first African American ever to be so confirmed. Although the position was a great honor, some blacks considered it beneath him. Douglass later appointed his son Lewis Henry as his second deputy.

In May 1878, in recognition of his prestigious postion, none other than Thomas Auld, his former master, respectfully addressed him as "Marshal Douglass."

Douglass visited with Auld in St. Michaels, Maryland. Auld had been stricken with palsy and was bedridden. "The sight of him," Douglass later wrote, "the changes which time had wrought in him, his tremulous hands constantly in motion, and all the circumstances of his condition affected me deeply, and for a time choked my voice and made me speechless." Auld cried and then told the man who had run away forty years before, "I always knew you were too smart to be a slave, and had I been in your place, I should have done as you did." And Douglass told his old master, "I did not run from *you*, but from *slavery*."

In 1881, Douglass visited the Lloyd estate, where he had experienced his first bitter taste of slavery. He was warmly greeted there by Howard Lloyd, the great-grandson of Colonel Edward Lloyd. The visit, Douglass wrote, "was one which could happen to but few men, and only once in the life time of any." The estate was much the same as Douglass remembered it. "Very little was missing except the squads of little black children which were once seen in all directions, and the great number of slaves in its fields."

Douglass looked in the kitchen where Aunt Katy had tormented him and where he had last seen his mother. He went to the window where Miss Lucretia sat, where she would give him bread when he was hungry. He was then invited to the great house, the place he described in his first autobiography as "a treat to my young and gradually opening mind to behold." Now, here he was more than fifty years later, sitting on its grand porch looking out at its garden filled with flowers and fruit trees, and drinking fine wine in the elegant dining room.

Next he visited Mrs. Ann Catherine Buchanan, one of Colonel Lloyd's daughters. "She invited me to a seat by her side," Douglass wrote, "introduced me to her grandchildren and conversed with me as freely and with as little embarrassment as if I had been an old acquaintance and occupied an equal station with the most aristocratic of the Caucasian race." Douglass felt that the experience told him "a new dispensation of justice, kindness, and human brotherhood was dawning not only in the North, but in the South."

Although Douglass saw great progress in the struggle for the civil rights of African Americans, he also knew how far they were from true equal treatment in America. "No white man, however friendly he may be," he said in a speech to Sunday school students in Washington, D.C., just three months after his visit with Mrs. Buchanan, "can see and feel the disadvantages under which we labor as well as he who wears the hated complexion."

In the same speech he said, "We are young in liberty and old in slavery. . . . We must leap over the many obstructions in our pathway and push onward; there must be no pausing; we must overcome them by action; and overcome bad acts by good acts; we must conquer prejudice by proper deportment in our daily walks."

President Rutherford B. Hayes

Cedar Hill, the Douglasses' home in Washington, D.C.

THE AFRICAN AMERICAN: "LIKE A MAN IN A MORASS"

The White-Leaguers came, cavalry, infantry, and artillery,
and they drove the colored men before them,
and compelled them to fly for their lives.
—FROM AN 1875 LETTER WRITTEN BY A WHITE REPUBLICAN

Iₙ 1878, Anna and Frederick Douglass and their daughter Rosetta and her family moved to a large, elegant home on a hill in Washington, D.C., with a view of the Capitol. Douglass named the house Cedar Hill because of the many cedar trees on the property. In a bit of irony, the land the house was built on had once been owned by General Robert E. Lee, commander of the Confederate army.

Douglass loved his new home. It had enough room for his children and grandchildren to visit. And he could walk to work. On Sunday afternoons, he and young visitors sometimes played croquet in the yard. He played his violin in the west parlor and insisted that his guests sing along. In the east parlor, he played checkers with his neighbors.

In 1880, James A. Garfield of Ohio was elected president. If Douglass was to keep his job as marshal, he would have to be reappointed. People campaigned against him. "The real ground of opposition to me is that I am a colored man," Douglass wrote Garfield, "and that my sympathies are with my recently enslaved people."

President James A. Garfield

Others campaigned for his reappointment.

In early 1881, Samuel Clemens wrote to President Garfield "as a simple citizen," though he was not so simple a citizen. He was the great author better known by his pseudonym, Mark Twain. "I beg permission to hope that you will retain Mr. Douglass in his present office as Marshall of the District of Columbia . . . because I so honor this man's high and blemishless character and so admire his brave, long crusade for the liberties and elevation of his race."

The next year, Garfield appointed one of his friends to the job and made Douglass Recorder of Deeds for Washington, D.C.

In mid-July 1882, Douglass wrote to a friend that his wife, Anna, was so gravely ill that she was "pressing near the gates of death." Her left side was paralyzed, the result of a stroke. When she died on August 4, Douglass wrote, "The main pillar of my house has fallen." After the funeral, Douglass, his daughter Rosetta, and granddaughter Annie returned to Rochester, where Anna was buried.

"My life has been more of cloud than sunshine," Douglass said a few months later, "more of storm than calm, it has nevertheless been a cheerful life." He went on to say: "He would be a gloomy man indeed who could live to see the desire of his soul accomplished, and yet spend his life in grief."

At a dinner held in his honor and celebrating the twentieth anniversary of Lincoln's Emancipation Proclamation, Douglass said, "I can say of the colored man's liberty I have rocked it in its cradle and witnessed its manhood, for I stand in the presence of emancipated millions."

A year later, on January 24, 1884, Douglass brought more sunshine to his life. But with it, again, came more storm than calm. He married Helen Pitts, a forty-six-year-old college-educated woman who had been a secretary in his Recorder of Deeds office. What brought the storm was her color. She was white.

The marriage was criticized by blacks who saw it as Douglass's abandonment of his race. His own children did not approve of the marriage and did not attend the ceremony. Whites objected, too. Douglass and Helen went to visit her family, but her father would not let his black son-in-law in the house. A Virginia newspaper described Douglass as a "lecherous old African Solomon."

Douglass told his critics that Anna, his first wife, "was the color of my mother" and Helen, his second wife, "the color of my father." He also reminded people that he fought his whole life so that people would not be judged by the color of their skin or by their gender. Wouldn't it be an act of prejudice, he reasoned, if he refused to marry Helen Pitts because she was white?

"Love came to me," Helen Pitts Douglass simply explained, "and I was not afraid to marry the man I loved because of his color."

That fall, in the 1884 presidential election, Douglass supported James G. Blaine of Maine, the Republican candidate, but it was the Democrat, Grover Cleveland of New York, who was elected.

"He is not a snob," Douglass wrote of Cleveland. "He is not a coward." In the country there was still a lot of antiblack sentiment, and Cleveland had the courage to invite Douglass and his wife to the White House for formal dinners.

Helen Pitts Douglass

President Grover Cleveland

He let Douglass keep his job as Recorder of Deeds for another year, but in January 1886, at Cleveland's request, Douglass resigned.

Douglass was now free to travel, and in September 1886 he and Helen sailed to Europe. In England, they visited Anna and Ellen Richardson, the women who had bought his freedom from Hugh Auld. "It was a great privilege," he later wrote, "once more to look into the faces and hear the voices of these noble and benevolent women."

The Douglasses also visited France, Italy, Greece, and Egypt, where he saw what he called the "living locomotive of the east," a line of camels. "I have a large sympathy with all burden-bearers," he wrote, "whether they be men or beasts. . . . I was glad right here in the edge of Egypt to have a visible illustration of these qualities of the animal. I saw him kneel and saw the heavy load of sand put on his back; I saw him try to rise under its weight and heard his sad moan. I had at the moment much the same feeling as when I first saw a gang of slaves chained together and shipped to a foreign market."

The long line of camels moving slowly over the seemingly endless desert gave Douglass an impression of how the land must have been in Biblical times. "In this wide waste," he wrote, "under this cloudless sky, star-lighted by night and by a fierce blazing sun by day, where even the wind seems voiceless, it was natural for men to look up to the sky and stars and contemplate the universe and infinity above and around them."

Perhaps, too, in this quiet place, the almost seventy-year-old Douglass, a religious man, was thinking of his own mortality. He wrote that "the heart beats louder and the soul hears quicker in silence and solitude."

With some help, he climbed to the top of the tallest pyramid, Cheops. He stood there looking at the other pyramids, the Sphinx, and the desert beyond. "There are stirred in the one who beholds it for the first time," he wrote, "thoughts and feelings never thought and felt before." While nothing would tempt him to make the climb again, he was "very glad to have had the experience once, and once is enough for a lifetime."

Douglass traveled for almost a full year, returning to the United States in

Facing page: Frederick Douglass with one of his grandson

August 1887. Helen went home earlier, in June, to be with her mother, who was ill.

In March 1888, Douglass traveled again. This time he went south, to Charleston, South Carolina, and Augusta, Georgia. He was dismayed by the poverty he found among African Americans, seeing that they were "systematically and universally cheated." For many, their wages of just eight dollars a month was given in credit at a store owned by their white employers, where they were "often made to pay a double price" for food and clothing. The black worker, he said in a talk, was "like a man in a morass, the more he struggles, the deeper he sinks." There were also all sorts of voting laws that kept African Americans out of the political process.

"Shame, eternal shame," he said, on anyone who criticized the free blacks who lived in poverty. Southern landowners and both the local and national governments had abandoned the African American and left him "a deserted, a defrauded, a swindled, and an outcast man."

Douglass felt the real power for reform was in the voting booth, that African Americans needed to be granted full suffrage. In June 1888, he went to Chicago, to the Republican National Convention. In his address to the delegates, he implored them to remember that the brave black men who fought during the Civil War "are now stripped of their constitutional right to vote. . . . [E]xtend over them the protecting arm of this government, and make their pathway to the ballot-box as straight and as smooth and as safe as that of any other class of citizens."

The cause of African American suffrage was included in the party platform. The Republican candidate, Benjamin Harrison of Indiana, endorsed it, and a satisfied Frederick Douglass joined the campaign. He traveled through five states and spoke day and night, in skating rinks and public halls, for the election of Harrison.

In November, with 100,000 fewer votes than Grover Cleveland, the Democratic Party's candidate, but with a majority in the Electoral College, Harrison was elected president. On July 1, 1889, Harrison appointed Douglass as Minister Resident and Consul-General to the Republic of Haiti.

President Benjamin Harrison

Chapter Fifteen ✳

"FROM FIRST TO LAST— A NOBLE LIFE"

There never walked a grander man than he!
He was a peer of princes—yea, a king!
—From *Sonnets to the Memory of*
Frederick Douglass, THEODORE TILTON,
MARCH 1895

I‍T WAS "with many misgivings," Frederick Douglass wrote to a friend, that he accepted the post of Minister Resident and Consul-General to the Republic of Haiti. "I distrusted my qualifications for the office; but coming to me as it did, unasked, unsought, and unexpected, and with the earnest wish of the President that I would accept it in the interest of the peace, welfare, and prosperity of Hayti (sic), I felt I could not decline it."

In September 1889, Douglass and Helen traveled to Norfolk, Virginia, and sailed from there on a government steamship, the *Ossipee,* to Haiti. The captain refused to eat with an African American, and Douglass refused to be treated with any less respect than any other U.S. diplomat, so it was the captain who ate elsewhere. Douglass and Helen dined without him in the officers' dining room.

President Louis Mondestin Florvil Hyppolite welcomed Douglass to Haiti. "Your reputation is known in the two hemispheres," he said. "You are the

An engraving of President Louis Mondestin Florvil Hyppolite of Haiti, from an 1888 issue of Harper's Weekly

incarnation of the idea which Haiti is following—the moral and intellectual development of the African race."

It was President Harrison's hope that Douglass could get permission for the United States to build a naval base on the island. He couldn't. The reason for Haiti's refusal was the nation's strong desire to remain fully independent. But many people blamed Douglass.

"One of the charitable apologies they are pleased to make for my failure is my color," Douglass wrote in 1892. "This color argument is not new. It besieged the White House before I was appointed. . . . I defy any man to prove, by any word or act of the Haitian Government, that I was less respected at the capital of Haiti than was any white minister or consul."

Indeed, President Hyppolite greatly respected Douglass. In 1893, well after Douglass had left his post as minister, he was asked by Hyppolite to serve as the Haitian commissioner at the World's Columbian Exposition in Chicago. Douglass described his roles as minister to Haiti and Haitian commissioner to the Exposition as "crowning honors to my long career and a fitting and happy close to my whole public life."

On May 31, 1891, just three days after a brief but frightening rebel attack in Port-au-Prince, the capital city of Haiti, Douglass applied for a leave from his post as minister so that he could return to his home in Washington, D.C. Helen was ill, and he didn't enjoy Haiti's tropical climate. Two months later, after less than two years in office, he resigned for "personal reasons."

Douglass returned to an uproar over lynchings in the United States. There were more than two hundred in 1892. Most of the victims were black men in the South. These violent murders by mobs were one way whites tried to reestablish their dominance. Ida B. Wells, a black journalist from Tennessee, launched a crusade against lynching. The Reverend G. H. N. Smith, a former minister to Haiti, declared in February 1893 in a New York City church: "The time has come when the colored people should take action against such outrages." He said, "All those in favor of forming an association for that object will rise," and everyone stood.

Douglass blamed not just the mobs, who, he wrote, "simply obey the public sentiment," but also the "respectable" people of the South who encouraged them.

Between 1882 and 1892, more than 1,400 blacks were lynched. In 1892 the Republican Party denounced lynchings as "inhuman outrages." Tragically, these violent acts continued well into the twentieth century.

By the time Douglass returned from Haiti, he was already in his midseventies. But he remained active in many of the same causes he had always championed.

On February 20, 1895, he attended a women's rights meeting that was held just a mile from his home. When he entered the room, everyone stood to honor him. They cheered and waved their handkerchiefs as he sat by the dais beside his friend Susan B. Anthony. No one noticed anything unusual about his appearance that day except that, according to one woman, he constantly rubbed his left hand, as if it was numb.

A lynching

At about 5 p.m. he left the hall. He had dinner with Helen and told her about the day's meetings. He became agitated in his descriptions, and with his hands clasped, he fell to his knees. At first, Helen thought he was mimicking one of the speakers, but then he fell to the floor, and she knew he was ill. She rushed to the front door and called for help.

Frederick Douglass died that night at about seven o'clock in the hallway of his home. He was seventy-seven years old.

The nation mourned its fallen hero.

People throughout the country sent telegrams of sympathy to Helen. A *Washington Post* editorial called Douglass "one of the great men of the century . . . in the triumph of the abolition crusade, no leader in the fight was more potent."

"From first to last his was a noble life," declared the *London Daily News*. "His own people have lost a father and a friend, and all good men have lost a comrade in the fight for the legal emancipation of one race and the spiritual emancipation of all."

On Monday, February 25, the day of his funeral, African American lower schools, high schools, and Howard University, a school founded after the Civil War to educate former slaves, closed to honor his memory. Businesses owned by blacks closed, too.

Frederick Douglass's open coffin was taken to the altar of Washington's African Methodist Episcopal Church. It was set in the midst of the many floral tributes sent by friends, schools, and the Haitian government. Thousands of men and women cried openly as they quietly walked past it. Parents lifted their children to see the face of their champion. Among the mourners were two young African American girls who stopped and placed a small bunch of white flowers beside the casket.

"Did you know him?" someone asked. "Oh, no, sir," the elder of the girls replied, "but Papa told us how he had labored all his life that we might be free and happy. We are so grateful for I was reading *Uncle Tom's Cabin* when Mr. Douglass died." The novel written by Harriet Beecher Stowe had awakened the nation in the 1850s to the horrors of slavery.

At the funeral, President Jeremiah Rankin of Howard University compared Douglass to the biblical Joseph, who was sold into slavery in Egypt that he might later rescue his brothers. "It was not the least of Frederick Douglass' fortunes," Rankin said, "that he was born in slavery. How otherwise could he have accomplished the work that was mapped out for him?"

Douglass's pastor, the Reverend J. T. Jenifer, said at the funeral, "Today the world unites in sympathy with us who sorrow for our great loss, by this death. . . . We mourn the taking away of him who was our eminent and loved leader, and most illustrious example of our possibilities as a people, Frederick

An engraving of Frederick Douglass in his district marshal's office in Washington, D.C., from an 1879 issue of Harper's Weekly

Douglass, a representative, ever faithful to his people, their champion, wise counselor, and fearless defender. Such a life as his is itself an oration, and this gathering an echo."

What would Douglass have said to the thousands who gathered that day? Perhaps he would have repeated what he wrote in an 1879 letter that acknowledged a bust of him being placed in the University of Rochester. "Incidents of this character do much amaze me. . . . It is not, however, the height to which I have risen, but the depth from which I have come, that amazes me."

"I remember that God reigns in eternity," he said in an 1890 speech, "and that whatever delays, whatever disappointments and discouragements may come, truth, justice, liberty, and humanity will ultimately prevail."

Frederick Douglass was buried on February 26, 1895, in Mount Hope Cemetery in Rochester, New York.

IMPORTANT DATES IN THE LIFE
OF FREDERICK DOUGLASS

Frederick Douglass

1818   Born in Talbot County, Maryland, February. His mother names him Frederick Augustus Washington Bailey.

1824   Taken to live in the slave quarters of the Lloyd plantation, August.

1825   Sees his mother, Harriet Bailey, for the last time.

1826   Sent to Baltimore, Maryland, to be the slave of Sophia and Hugh Auld.

1827   Sophia Auld teaches him to read.

1833   Sent to St. Michaels, Maryland, to work for Thomas Auld, March.

1834   Sent to work for Edward Covey, a notorious "slave breaker." Covey beats him several times until Douglass fights back.

1835   Works for William Freeland. Douglass makes a failed attempt to escape. Sent back to Hugh Auld in Baltimore.

1837   Meets Anna Murray.

1838   Escapes to New York, September 3. Marries Anna Murray, September 15.

1839   Daughter Rosetta born, June 24.

1840   Son Lewis Henry born, October 9.

1841   Gives first speech at antislavery meeting on Nantucket, August.

1842   Son Frederick Jr. born, March 3.

1843   Beaten by a mob at an antislavery meeting in Pendleton, Indiana, September.

1844   Son Charles Remond born, October 21.

1845   Autobiographical *Narrative of the Life of Frederick Douglass, an American Slave* is published. Goes on speaking tour of England.

1846   Buys his freedom from Hugh Auld and is no longer a fugitive slave.

1847   Moves to Rochester, New York, and begins publishing *The North Star*, an abolitionist weekly newspaper.

1848   Attends women's rights convention at Seneca Falls, New York. His home becomes a stop on the Underground Railroad.

1849   Daughter Annie born, March 22.

1855   *My Bondage and My Freedom*, an updated autobiography, is published.

1859   Secretly meets with John Brown, August 20. Brown and his followers seize federal arsenal at Harpers Ferry, Virginia, October 16. Douglass leaves for England, November 12. John Brown executed, December 2.

1860   Daughter Annie dies, March 13.

1861   The Civil War begins.

1863   The Emancipation Proclamation, freeing all slaves in states controlled by the Confederate Army, becomes law, January 1.
        Meets President Abraham Lincoln and complains of poor treatment of African American soldiers in the Union army, August 10.

1865   President Lincoln is killed, April 14. Thirteenth Amendment to the Constitution is ratified; slavery is now illegal in all states.

1866   Meets with President Andrew Johnson, asks for his support for black suffrage, February 7.

1870   Becomes editor of a Washington weekly newspaper, *The New National Era*.

1872   The Equal Rights Party nominates Victoria C. Woodhull for president of the United States and Douglass for vice president. Home in Rochester is destroyed by fire, June 2.

1874   Becomes president of Freedman's Savings and Trust Company, March 14.

1877   Appointed United States Marshal.

1881   Visits the Lloyd estate and meets with Lloyd's daughter, Mrs. Ann Catherine Buchanan, June. *The Life and Times of Frederick Douglass*, his third autobiography, is published, November.

1882   Wife Anna Murray Douglass dies, August 4.

1884   Marries Helen Pitts, January 24.

1886   Sails with Helen to England, September.

1888   Travels to South Carolina and Georgia, March.

1889   Appointed United States minister to Haiti, July 1.

1895   Dies of heart attack, February 20.

PREFACE

"No man . . . high.""Greatness of Douglass," *New York Times*, February 25, 1895, p. 7.

"father of . . . movement." Foner, Frederick Douglass qouting *Ebony*, September 1963.

CHAPTER ONE:
"I Sobbed Myself to Sleep"

Douglass wrote of Stowe's book, *Uncle Tom's Cabin*, "No book on the subject of slavery had so generally and favorably touched the American heart." *Life and Times*, p. 271.

p. 1   "I hate him . . . to the ground." Stowe, p. 514.
p. 1   "Work, work . . . of the day." *Life and Times*, p. 104.
p. 1   "completely wrecked . . . almost to madness." *My Bondage*, p. 221.
p. 1   "*Are you going* . . . Yes sir." *My Bondage*, p. 243.
p. 2   "I would not have . . . *not whipped me at all.*" *My Bondage*, p. 246.
p. 2   "I was *nothing* . . . A MAN NOW." *My Bondage*, p. 246.
p. 3   "She would . . . was gone." *Narrative*, p. 14.
p. 3   "enjoyed the . . . little children." *My Bondage*, p. 35.

p. 3   "My grandmother . . . her return." *My Bondage*, p. 40.
p. 4   "is never chided . . . runs wild." *My Bondage*, p. 41.
p. 4   "The journey . . . her shoulder." *Life and Times*, p. 6.
p. 3   "Grandmamma looked . . . not the cause." *My Bondage*, p. 47.
p. 4   "of many colors . . . to you." *My Bondage*, p. 47.
p. 4   "Slavery . . . strangers." *My Bondage*, p. 48.
p. 4   "Fed, Fed, Grandmamma gone!" *Life and Times*, p. 7.
p. 4   "but I . . . to sleep." *My Bondage*, p. 49.

CHAPTER TWO:
"Many Children but No Family"

Douglass saw the stingy rations given slaves lead to tragedy. He wrote in his autobiography *Narrative of the Life of Frederick Douglass, an American Slave* (p. 27) of an old slave who was fishing for oysters and wandered off the property. The neighbor, Mr. Beal Bondly, saw the man and shot him. The next day Bondly visited Lloyd, either to explain why he had killed his slave or to pay Lloyd for the loss. "At any rate," Douglass wrote, "the whole fiendish transaction was soon hushed up. There was very little said about it at all, and nothing done." It was a common saying then among whites that it was "worth half a cent to kill" a black "and half a cent to bury one."

p. 5   "The very earliest . . . alive or not." *Slave Testimony*, p. 616.

p. 5   "was a treat . . . and beauty." *Autobiographies*, p. 488.

p. 6   "filled the Great . . . tempt the taste." *Life and Times*, pp. 34–35.

p. 6   "purple and fine linen." *Life and Times*, p. 34.

p. 6   "The table . . . and abroad." *Autobiographies*, p. 190.

p. 6   "unending round of feasting." *Autobiographies*, p. 191.

p. 6   "the teeming . . . delicious cream." *Autobiographies*, p. 190.

p. 6   "The greatest . . . of the south." *Narrative*, p. 21.

p. 6   "This plan . . . of the lash." *Narrative*, p. 21.

p. 8   "like so many . . . devour the mush." *Life and Times*, p. 49.

p. 8   "More slaves . . . other fault." *My Bondage*, p. 102.

p. 8   "'Well, boy . . . as it is.'" *Autobiographies*, p. 196.

p. 8   "*This is the . . . plain questions.*" *Autobiographies*, p. 197.

p. 8   "ambitious . . . cruel." *My Bondage*, p. 74.

p. 9   "Want of food . . . for the cats." *My Bondage*, pp. 75–76.

p. 9   "her favorite . . . after breakfast." *Autobiographies*, p. 153.

p. 9   "Sundown came, but no bread." *Autobiographies*, p. 154.

p. 9   "The friendless . . . a mother." *My Bondage*, p. 56.

p. 10   "That night . . . upon his throne." *Life and Times*, p. 10.

p. 10   "I was not allowed . . . about it." *Narrative*, p. 14.

p. 10   "My poor . . . no family!" *My Bondage*, p. 48.

CHAPTER THREE:
"Why Am I a Slave?"

Austin Gore may have been Orson Gore, as there is a tombstone in Easton, Maryland, with that name and the dates 1794–1871.

In his autobiographies, Douglass gives his aunt's name as both Hester and Esther.

p. 11   "was noted . . . when a baby." *Slave Testimony*, p. 236.

p. 12   "Everybody in . . . somebody else." *Autobiographies*, p. 491.

p. 12   "Say everything . . . come the lash." *Autobiographies*, p. 165.

p. 12   "There was even . . . and punishment." *Life and Times*, p. 18.

p. 12   "The slaveholder . . . slave system." *Life and Times*, p. 21.

p. 12   "Could the reader . . . old man." *Autobiographies*, p. 172.

p. 12   "commit outrages . . . and nameless," *Life and Times*, p. 21.

p. 12   "an army of invisible foes." *Autobiographies*, p. 172.

p. 13   "tall, well formed . . . fine appearence." "is ever a curse . . . slave-girl." "fine looking." *Autobiographies*, p. 175.

p. 13   "It was early . . . increase his fury." "terrified . . . and bewildered." *Life and Times*, pp. 24–25.

p. 14   "Let my mammy . . . go!" *Autobiographies*, p. 500.

p. 14   "He was whipped . . . a freeman." *Life and Times*, pp. 28–29.

p. 14 "Why am I . . . others masters?" *My Bondage,* p. 89.

p. 14 "I have nothing . . . of this sort." *My Bondage,* p. 129.

p. 16 "was nothing to Baltimore." *Life and Times,* p. 51.

p. 16 "I had been treated . . . a *child* now." *My Bondage,* p. 142.

p. 17 "I speak within . . . give you more." "They seldom knew . . . into the street." *Autobiographies,* pp. 219–20.

p. 18 "Men and women . . . and slaveholder." *My Bondage,* p. 175.

p. 18 "attended with fear and dread." *My Bondage,* p. 176.

p. 18 "I could see . . . hold of me." *My Bondage,* p. 178.

CHAPTER FOUR:
"The Turning Point"

p. 19 "All these creatures . . . kept in order." Stowe, p. 487.

p. 19 "should know nothing . . . told to do." "no keeping him." *Narrative,* p. 31.

p. 20 "I finally found that . . . new light." *My Bondage,* p. 166.

p. 20 "often wished . . . to be happy." *My Bondage,* p. 160.

p. 20 "I saw nothing . . . in every storm." *My Bondage,* p. 160.

p. 20 "she was considered . . . to Baltimore." *Life and Times,* p. 80.

p. 21 "If he cannot . . . have Fred." *My Bondage,* p. 182.

p. 21 "I frankly confess . . . find it." *My Bondage,* pp. 188–89.

p. 21 "taking his meat . . . into another." *My Bondage,* p. 189.

p. 21 "If he has . . . more kindly." *Life and Times,* p. 87.

p. 22 "all living . . . nearly starving." *My Bondage,* p. 198.

p. 22 "There was not . . . Mr. Cookman." *Autobiographies,* p. 558.

p. 22 "in a manner . . . and shocking." "turning loose . . . to starve and die." *My Bondage,* p. 201.

p. 24 "We worked all . . . long for him." *Life and Times,* 104.

p. 24 "If you have . . . cure you." *My Bondage,* p. 225.

p. 24 "allow this . . . marred and defaced." *Autobiographies,* p. 273.

p. 24 "deserved it." *Narrative,* p. 52.

p. 25 "Both seemed . . . brother slaves." *My Bondage,* p. 237.

p. 25 "fighting madness." *My Bondage,* p. 242.

p. 25 "was frightened . . . or blows." *My Bondage,* p. 244.

p. 25 "He had not . . . from me." *My Bondage,* p. 246.

CHAPTER FIVE:
"You Rascal!"

James W. C. Pennington was an African American enslaved in Maryland. He escaped in the late 1820s to become a teacher and the minister who officiated at the 1838 wedding of Frederick Douglass and Anna Murray.

p. 4 "How can I expect . . . Maryland ends." Bayliss, p. 197.

p. 4 "Give him . . . his *own* master." *My Bondage,* p. 263.

p. 4 "some sense . . . feelings of humanity." *My Bondage,* p. 257.

p. 4 "up to my old tricks." *My Bondage,* p. 264.

p. 4 "This is . . . Easter holidays." *Autobiographies,* p. 314.

p. 4 "It is all over . . . betrayed." *My Bondage,* p. 290.

p. 4 "Cross your hands . . . be tied." *Autobiographies,* p. 616.

p. 4 "You devil . . . running away." *My Bondage,* p. 330.

p. 4 "They laughed . . . haven't we?" *Autobiographies,* p. 620.

p. 4 "was almost . . . murderous assault." *My Bondage,* p. 315.

p. 4 "Mr. Auld . . . you speak." "I am sorry . . . white witnesses." *My Bondage,* pp. 316–17.

p. 4 "If I had . . . single murderer." *My Bondage,* p. 317.

p. 4 "Lay out . . . care of you." *Autobiographies,* pp. 636–37.

p. 4 "You rascal! . . . your running away." *My Bondage,* p. 330.

p. 4 "So well pleased . . . good use of it.'" *My Bondage,* p. 333.

CHAPTER SIX:
New Bedford: "I Had No Master"

The Reverend Henry H. Garnet escaped slavery at the age of eleven.

p. 4 "Brethren, arise . . . be slaves!" Katz, pp. 176–77.

p. 4 "I suppose . . . the world." *Life and Times,* p. 182.

p. 4 "I really . . . betray me." *Life and Times,* p. 183.

p. 4 "minutes were . . . hours were days." *Life and Times,* p. 182.

p. 4 "I was indeed . . . shelter as well." *Life and Times,* p. 187.

p. 4 "I could . . . contrast." *Life and Times,* p. 193.

p. 4 "everything managed . . . and strength." *Life and Times,* p. 191.

p. 4 "What will . . . madam." *Life and Times,* p. 193.

p. 4 "swelled . . . realising . . . that I had . . . precious coin." *Autobiographies,* p. 654.

p. 4 "It detested . . . from bondage." *Life and Times,* p. 197.

CHAPTER SEVEN:
The Lecture Circuit: "I Can Tell You What I Have Seen"

p. 4 "Slavery has . . . this generation." Ruchames, p. 245.

p. 4 "the resurrection . . . buried hopes." "The style of . . . be counterfeited." Holland, p. 43.

p. 4 "I will . . . *be heard.*" *The Liberator,* January 1, 1831.

p. 4 "Why are you . . . to melt." Holland, p. 45.

p. 4 "It was common . . . Negro slavery." Bartlett, p. 45.

p. 4 "the utmost . . . stammering." *Life and Times,* p. 199.

p. 4 "In a few moments . . . such powers." Bartlett, p. 45.

p. 4 "Have we been . . . No, no!" Holland, pp. 58–59.

p. 4 "I shall never . . . at that moment." Gregory, p. 98.

p. 4 "a commanding . . . quite elegant." Holland, pp. 63–64.

p. 4 "as men . . . remarkable man." Foner, p. 47

p. 4 "He had just . . . his tongue." Holland, p. 82.

p. 4 "It has . . . heard him." *The Liberator*, June 17, 1842, in Foner, p. 52.

p. 4 "thing . . . Southern property." *Life and Times*, p. 201.

p. 4 "I feel greatly . . . good Christian." Blassingame, p. 3.

p. 4 "People in . . . don't know more." Ritchie, p. 41.

p. 4 "Douglass, if you cannot . . . with you." Foner, p. 53.

p. 4 "What can I . . . you say, please?" Holland, pp. 96–97.

p. 4 "many persons . . . to devise." *The Liberator*, August 31, 1844.

p. 4 "He's never . . . warrant you." Holland, p. 102.

p. 4 "I can tell you . . . that man." Blassingame, pp. 29–31.

p. 4 "While you continue . . . the slaveholder." Blassingame, p. 33.

p. 4 "Some years ago . . . into the fire." Holland, p. 102.

CHAPTER EIGHT:
"From House to House, and from Heart to Heart"

p. 4 "Go where we . . . contend against." Katz, p. 159.

p. 4 "My readers . . . heart to heart." *The Liberator*, May 30, 1845.

p. 4 "Mr. Thompson . . . own opinion." "the evidence . . . ranting negro." *The Liberator*, February 20, 1846.

p. 4 "I have seen . . . villainous fabrication." *The Liberator*, February 20, 1846.

p. 4 "the statements . . . basely false." *The Liberator*, February 20, 1846.

p. 4 "He states . . . to do it." *The Liberator*, February 20, 1846.

p. 4 "I am greatly . . . the slave." *The Liberator*, February 27, 1846.

p. 4 "The insult . . . in steerage." *Life and Times*, p. 219.

p. 4 "I can truly say . . . of my skin." *Life and Times*, p. 230.

p. 4 "Would master Hugh . . . hold of me." Foner, p. 72.

p. 4 "I acted from necessity." *The Liberator*, January 29, 1847.

p. 4 "upwards of . . . great respectability." *The Liberator*, April 30, 1847.

p. 4 "Mr. Douglass visited . . . of slavery." *The Liberator*, April 30, 1847.

p. 4 "I have traveled . . . of my color." Holland, p. 145.

p. 4 "'Pro-Slavery . . . of Color.'" Foner, p. 75.

CHAPTER NINE:
"What, to the American Slave, Is Your 4th of July?"

p. 4 "You like . . . disenfranchised class." Katz, p. 180.

p. 4 "I am here . . . be devised." Foner, *Selected Speeches*, pp. 76–77.

p. 60 "Mr. President . . . anniversary." Foner, *Selected Speeches*, pp. 193–194.

p. 7 "What . . . very hour." Foner, *Selected Speeches*, p. 196.

p. 61 "I do not . . . jubilee." Foner, *Selected Speeches*, p. 197.

p. 7 "In imagination . . . to the grave." *Life and Times*, p. 246.

p. 7 "contribute another . . . of my race." *Life and Times*, p. 246.

p. 7 "I know . . . and cooperation." In *The Crooked Lake Review*, an online newsletter, fall 2005, http://www.crookedlakereview.com/articles/136_167/137fall2005/137shilling.html

p. 7 "Of all the stars . . . fellow countrymen." *The North Star*, December 3, 1847.

p. 7 "was fortunate . . . Mrs. Douglass." Holland, p. 226.

p. 7 "He has a . . . common sense." Holland, p. 225.

p. 7 "I am . . . a father." Foner, p. 136.

p. 7 "but never . . . his audience." Holland, p. 261.

p. 7 "cheerfulness and refinement." Holland, p. 250.

p. 7 "in recognition . . . Anti-slavery cause." McFeely, p. 322.

p. 7 "If there ever . . . strike him down." *The North Star*, January 23, 1851.

p. 7 "whose character . . . heart and mind." *Life and Times*, p. 259.

p. 7 "forfeited their right to live." *Life and Times*, p. 261.

p. 7 "Our doctrine . . . humble Godspeed." Holland, p. 171.

p. 7 "We differ in color . . . honorable feeling." Foner, p. 128.

CHAPTER TEN:
"Foreshadowed a Conflict
on a Larger Scale"

p. 7 "Whether my time . . . prepared to go." Lossing, vol. 1, p. 419.

p. 7 "as a means . . . satisfactory work." *Life and Times*, p. 254.

p. 7 "I returned . . . to describe." *Autobiographies*, p. 726.

p. 7 "To me . . . and murderers." Foner, p. 133.

p. 7 "This bill . . . gives away." *Frederick Douglass' Paper*, November 10, 1854.

p. 7 "Southern ladies . . . larger scale." *Life and Times*, pp. 282–83.

p. 7 "We are now . . . cannot stand." Foner, *Selected Speeches*, pp. 347–48.

p. 7 "met persecution . . . a murderer."
"the logical result . . . persecutions." *Life and Times*, p. 291.

p. 7 "Our talk was . . . proposed by him.
"Come with me . . . help hive them." *Life and Times*, p. 309.

p. 7 "Are you . . . my designs." *The National Era*, October 27, 1859.

p. 7 "Gerrit Smith . . . Republicans Implicated." Foner, p. 179.

p. 7 "whose one right hand . . . in his own way." *The Liberator*, November 11, 1859.

p. 7 "Although vengeance . . . around your neck." *The Liberator*, December 16, 1859.

p. 7 "You are . . . of my mother." *National Era*, December 8, 1859.

CHAPTER ELEVEN:
"To Arms!"

p. 7 "No state . . . of the Union." Channing, p. 508.

p. 7 "the Constitution . . . the laws." McMaster, p. 363.

p. 7 "Into this . . . threw myself." *Life and Times*, p. 317.

p. 7 "a man . . . firmness of will." Foner, p. 184.

p. 7 "Still we . . . on the wave." *Life and Times*, p. 323.

p. 7 "To arms . . . be preserved." Andrews, p. 335.

p. 7 "There can be . . . and traitors." Andrews, p. 336.

p. 7 "For the moment . . . use them." *Life and Times*, p. 324.

p. 7 "On to Richmond!" Andrews, p. 353.

p. 7 "Since his inauguration . . . nothing more." *New York Herald*, December 12, 1861.

p. 7 "From the . . . end of slavery." *Life and Times*, p. 325.

p. 7 "The only . . . the Union." Holland, pp. 287–88.

p. 7 "with their soft . . . behind them." *Life and Times*, p. 326.

CHAPTER TWELVE:
"A Sacred Effort"

p. 7 "All persons held . . . forever free." Lossing, vol. 3, p. 225.

p. 7 "God Almighty's . . . of freedom!" *Washington Chronicle*, p. 375.

p. 7 "practically a dead letter." *New York Herald*, January 3, 1863.

p. 7 "What shall be done . . . to degrade him." Holland, pp. 292–93.

p. 7 "of suitable condition," http://www.yale.edu/ lawweb/avalon/emancipa.htm

p. 7 "Men of . . . its lustre." Holland, p. 297.

p. 7 "The old flag . . . the ground." *New York Times*, May 3, 1896, p. 26.

p. 7 "The attitude . . . and discouragement." *Life and Times*, p. 333.

p. 7 "I shall never . . . and tired." *Life and Times*, p. 337.

p. 7 "justice would . . . their promise." "positions of . . . perfect equality." *Life and Times*, p. 340.

p. 7 "fought with . . . all praise." *New York Times*, May 3, 1896, p. 26.

p. 7 "There is no . . . its chances." *New York Times*, May 3, 1896, p. 26.

p. 7 "Rich man's war, poor man's fight." *Washington Chronicle*, p. 379.

p. 7 "thieves, burglars . . . jailbirds." *New York Herald*, July 24, 1863.

p. 7 "my friends . . . his 'friends.'" *Life and Times*, p. 347.

p. 7 "There was a moral . . . due respect." *Life and Times*, p. 348.

p. 7 "What he said . . . written by him." *Life and Times*, p. 349.

p. 7 "years of failure . . . experiment of war." McMaster, p. 426.

p. 7 "I could not look . . . in vain." McMaster, p. 426.

p. 7 "There was a . . . of our race." *Life and Times*, pp. 355.

p. 7 "I have no . . . it exists." Lossing, vol. 5, p. 426.

p. 7 "It became . . . and calm." White, p. 42.

p. 7 "Fondly do we . . . with all nations." White, pp. 18–19.

p. 7 "I told the . . . President Lincoln." *Life and Times*, p. 357.

p. 7 "Here comes . . . more than yours." *Life and Times*, p. 357.

p. 7 "a sacred effort." *Life and Times*, p. 357.

p. 7 "complying with . . . of slavery." *Life and Times*, p. 357.

p. 7 "*great man* . . . unpopular color." *Life and Times*, p. 350.

p. 7 "I was called . . . made us 'kin.'" *Life and Times*, p. 363.

p. 7 "This is not . . . gentle eye." Kendrick, pp. 235–36.

p. 7 "I never heard . . . was done." Holland, p. 311.

CHAPTER THIRTEEN:
"Young in Liberty and Old in Slavery"

The Fifteenth Amendment to the Constitution declares that the right of all citizens to vote shall not be denied "on account of race, color, or previous condition of servitude." Following its passage, an African American minister wrote in a letter to a Pennsylvania newspaper, "The iron hoof of the tyrant is broken; the long bitter ages of injustice, blood, and whips are ended, and America's jubilee has come. For the first time in my life I write as an American citizen." (*Christian Recorder*, "Correspondence from Bishop Ward," May 12, 1870.)

p. 22 "I never . . . to learn." Katz, p. 238, and www.pbs.org/onlyateacher/charlotte.html.

p. 22 "a strange . . . longer needed." *Life and Times*, p. 364.

p. 23 "Where shall I go?" *Life and Times*, p. 364.

p. 23 "the wrongs . . . not ended." *Life and Times*, p. 368.

p. 23 "in some small measure helping." *Life and Times*, p. 368.

p. 23 "building up permanent . . . colored people." Holland, p. 314.

p. 23 "never . . . be reversed." Foner, p. 237.

p. 23 "not merely . . . enslaved class." *Life and Times*, pp. 369–70.

p. 23 "From the first . . . a citizen." *Life and Times*, p. 370.

p. 23 "was essential . . . the freedman."

p. 23 "As one learns . . . by voting." Foner, p. 239.

p. 23 "friends meeting a friend." Foner, p. 243.

p. 23 "The fact that . . . of this condition." Foner, p. 243.

p. 23 "from bondage . . . colored man." Foner, p. 243.

p. 23 "paraded . . . morning papers." *Life and Times,* p. 374.

p. 23 "Peace between . . . all classes." *Life and Times,* p. 376.

p. 23 "You might . . . this convention." Bergman, p. 251, *Life and Times,* p. 381.

p. 23 "I think . . . brave young man." *Life and Times,* p. 383.

p. 23 "I heard . . . this procession." *Life and Times,* p. 384.

p. 23 "This request . . . other ladies." *Life and Times,* p. 385.

p. 23 "If you will . . . and affection." *Life and Times,* p. 386.

p. 23 "Here was . . . great city." *Life and Times,* p. 384.

p. 23 "another and better world." *Life and Times,* p. 387.

p. 23 "an event . . . to describe." McFeely, p. 259.

p. 23 "I had small . . . was invited." *Life and Times,* pp. 390–91.

p. 23 "are objects . . . obtain the ballot." Foner, p. 265.

p. 23 "everything is possible to us." Miller, p. 121.

p. 23 "insolvent . . . was gone." *Life and Times,* pp. 397–98.

p. 23 "The sight of him . . . from *slavery." Autobiographies,* pp. 876–77.

p. 23 "was one which . . . of any." *Autobiographies,* p. 880.

p. 23 "Very little . . . in its fields." *Autobiographies,* p. 881.

p. 23 "a treat . . . to behold." *Autobiographies,* p. 488.

p. 23 "She invited . . . in the South." *Autobiographies,* p. 884.

p. 23 "No white man . . . our daily walks." *The Christian Recorder,* November 17, 1881.

CHAPTER FOURTEEN:
The African American:
"Like a Man in a Morass"

p. 23 "The White-Leaguers . . . for their lives." Katz, p. 269.

p. 23 "The real ground . . . enslaved people." Foner, p. 336.

p. 23 "as a simple . . . of his race." Foner, p. 336.

p. 23 "pressing near the gates of death." McFeely, p. 312.

p. 23 "The main . . . has fallen." Holland, p. 351.

p. 23 "My life . . . in grief."
"I can say . . . emancipated millions."
The Christian Recorder, January 11, 1883.

p. 23 "lecherous old African Solomon." Foner, p. 338: Miller, pp. 130–31.

p. 23 "was the color . . . my father." Foner, p. 338.

p. 23 "Love came to . . . of his color." Miller, p. 131.

p. 23 "He is not . . . a coward." Holland, p. 357.

p. 23 "It was a . . . benevolent women." *Autobiographies*, p. 988.

p. 23 "living locomotive . . . to a foreign market." *Autobiographies*, p. 1009.

p. 23 "In this wide . . . around them." *Autobiographies*, p. 1009.

p. 23 "the heart . . . and solitude." *Autobiographies*, p. 1010.

p. 23 "There are stirred . . . for a lifetime." *Autobiographies*, p. 1013.

p. 23 "systematically . . . cheated." Holland, p. 369

p. 23 "often made . . . double price." Foner, p. 332.

p. 23 "like a man . . . he sinks." Foner, p. 331.

p. 23 "Shame, eternal shame . . . outcast man." Foner, p. 332.

p. 23 "are now stripped . . . class of citizens." *Autobiographies*, p. 1020.

CHAPTER FIFTEEN:
"From First to Last—A Noble Life"

p. 23 "There never walked . . . yea, a king!" Chestnut, p. 58.

p. 23 "with many misgivings . . . not decline it." Holland, p. 383.

p. 23 "Your reputation . . . African race." Foner, p. 354.

p. 23 "One of the . . . minister or consul." *Autobiographies*, pp. 1027–28.

p. 23 "crowning honors . . . public life." *Autobiographies*, p. 1045.

p. 23 "The time has . . . will rise." *New York Times*, February 13, 1893, p. 9.

p. 23 "simply obey the public sentiment." Foner, p. 362.

p. 23 "inhuman outrages." Bergman, p. 309.

p. 23 "one of the great . . . more potent." *Washington Post*, February 22, 1895.

p. 23 "From first to last . . . emancipation of all." *New York Times*, February 22, 1895, p. 3.

p. 23 "Did you know . . . when Mr. Douglass died." *Washington Post*, February 26, 1895, p. 2.

p. 23 "It was not . . . for him." *Washington Post*, February 26, 1895.

p. 23 "Today the world . . . an echo." Gregory, p. 224.

p. 23 "Incidents of this . . . amazes me." *New York Times*, July, 2, 1879, quoting the *Rochester Democrat*, June 27, 1879.

p. 23 "I remember . . . ultimately prevail." *Washington Post*, October 22, 1890.

Frederick Douglass
at a lecture in March 1892

BOOKS

Andrews, E. Benjamin. *History of the United States,* vol. 3. New York: Scribners, 1904.

Bartlett, David W. *Modern Agitators: or Ten Portraits of Living American Reformers.* New York: Miller, Orton, and Mulligan, 1855.

Bayliss, John F. *Black Slave Narratives.* New York: Macmillan, 1970.

Bergman, Peter M. *The Chronological History of the Negro in America.* New York: Harper, 1969.

Blassingame, John W., ed. *Slave Testimony.* Baton Rouge: Louisiana State University Press, 1977.

———. *The Frederick Douglass Papers,* vol. 1. New Haven: Yale University Press, 1979.

Bontemps, Arna. *Free at Last: The Life of Frederick Douglass.* New York: Dodd, Mead, 1971.

Channing, Edward. *A Student's History of the United States.* New York: Macmillan, 1902.

Chronicle of America. Mount Kisco, NY: Chronicle, 1989.

Chestnut, Charles. *Frederick Douglass.* Mineola, NY: Dover, 2002.

Douglass, Frederick. *Autobiographies.* New York: Library of America, 1994.

———. *Life and Times of Frederick Douglass.* New York: Gramercy Books, 1993.

———. *My Bondage and My Freedom.* New York: Dover, 1969.

———. *Narrative of the Life of Frederick Douglass.* New Haven, CT: Yale University Press, 2001.

Foner, Philip S. *Frederick Douglass.* New York: Citadel Press, 1969.

———, ed. *Frederick Douglass: Selected Speeches and Writings.* Chicago: Lawrence Hill Books, 1975.

Goodrich, S. G. *Goodrich's Pictorial History of the United States.* Philadelphia: J. H. Butler, 1874.

Gregory, James M. *Frederick Douglass: The Orator.* Springfield, MA: Willey, 1893.

Holland, Frederic May. *Frederick Douglass: The Colored Orator.* New York: Funk and Wagnalls, 1891.

Katz, William Loren. *Eyewitness: The Negro in American History.* New York: Pitman, 1967.

Kendrick, Paul, and Stephen Kendrick. *Douglass and Lincoln.* New York: Walker, 2008.

Klagsbrun, Francine. *Freedom Now.* Boston: Houghton Mifflin, 1972.

Lossing, Benson John, ed. *Harper's Encyclopedia of United States History.* New York: Harper, 1907.

Macy, Jess. *The Anti-Slavery Crusade.* New Haven: Yale University Press, 1920.

Martin, James Kirby, Randy Roberts, Steven Mintz, Linda O. McMurry, and James H. Jones. *America and Its People.* New York: Harper, 1989.

McDougall, Walter A. *Throes of Democracy: The Civil War Era, 1829–1877*. New York: Harper, 2008.

McFeely, William S. *Frederick Douglass*. New York: Norton, 1991.

McMaster, John Bach. *A School History of the United States*. New York: American Book Company, 1897.

Meltzer, Milton. *Frederick Douglass: In His Own Words*. San Diego: Harcourt, 1995.

Miller, Douglas T. *Frederick Douglass and the Fight for Freedom*. New York: Facts on File, 1988.

Morison, Samuel Eliot, Henry Steele Commager, and William E. Leuchtenburg. *The Growth of the American Republic*. New York: Oxford University Press, 1969.

Noble, Edward M. *History of Caroline County, Maryland*. Frederalsburg, VA: J. W. Stowell, 1920.

Oakes, James. *The Radical and the Republican: Frederick Douglass, Abraham Lincoln, and the Triumph of Antislavery Politics*. New York: Norton, 2007.

Phillips, Rachael. *Frederick Douglass: Abolitionist and Reformer*. Thorndike, ME: Thorndike Press, 2000.

Ritchie, Barbara. *The Mind and Heart of Frederick Douglass*. New York: Crowell, 1968.

Ruchames, Louis. *The Abolitionist*. New York: Putnam, 1963.

Scholes, Percy A. *The Oxford Companion of Music*. London: Oxford University Press, 1955.

Stauffer, John. *The Black Hearts of Men: Radical Abolitionists and the Transformation of Race*. Cambridge: Harvard University Press, 2002.

Stowe, Harriet Beecher. *The Annotated Uncle Tom's Cabin*. Edited by Philip Van Doren Stern. New York: Paul S. Eriksson, Inc., 1964.

White, Ronald C., Jr. *Lincoln's Greatest Speech: The Second Inaugural*. New York: Simon & Schuster, 2002.

Newspapers

Christian Recorder, various issues, 1861–70, found at Accessible Archives, http://www.accessible.com/accessible/

Frederick Douglass' Paper, various issues, 1851–63, found at Accessible Archives.

The Liberator, various issues, 1831–65, found at Accessible Archives.

The National Era, various issues, 1847–60, found at Accessible Archives.

New York Herald, various issues, 1860–65, found at Accessible Archives.

New York Times, various issues, 1851–95.

The North Star, various issues, 1847–51, found at Accessible Archives.

Washington Post, various issues, 1890–95.

Andrews, E. Benjamin. *History of the United States*, volume 3. (New York: Scribners, 1904): pages 7, 15, 22, 35, 43, 65 (bottom)

Bartlett, W. H. *Bartlett's Classic Illustrations of America*. (Mineola, NY: Dover, 2000): pages 44, 57, 78

Carroll, Howard. *Twelve Americans: Their Lives and Times*. (New York: Harper & Brothers, Franklin Square, 1883): page 120

Dodd, William E. *The Cotton Kingdom: A Chronicle of the Old South*. (New Haven: Yale University Press, 1919): page 5

Channing, Edward. *A Student's History of the United States*. (New York: Macmillan, 1902): page 16

Estill, Harry F. *The Beginner's History of Our Country*. (Dallas, Texas: The Southern Publishing Company, 1916): page 83 (top)

Fiske, John. *A History of the United States for Schools*. (Boston, New York and Chicago: Houghton, Mifflin and Company, 1897): pages 1, 75, 83 (middle), 83 (bottom) 94, 95, 99, 105, 110, 112

Grafton, John. *The Civil War: A Concise History and Picture Sourcebook*. (Mineola, NY: 2003): pages 19, 95 (top), 115

Gregory, James M. *Frederick Douglass: The Orator*. (Springfield, MA: Willey, 1893): pages 102 (top and bottom), 103 (top and bottom), 106, 108, 114

Hosmer, James K. *A Short History of the Mississippi Valley*. (Boston and New York: Houghton, Mifflin and Company, 1901): page 84

Library of Congress, Rare Book and Special Collections Division: pages 16, 33, 96, 111, 130

Lossing, ed. Benson John. *Harper's Encyclopedia of United States History*. (New York: Harper, 1907): pages 64 (bottom), 65 (top), 95 (bottom), 96

Macy, Jess. *The Anti-Slavery Crusade*. (New Haven: Yale University Press, 1920): pages 37, 64 (top), 77, 93

Massaachusetts Historical Society: page 42

National Park Service: pages ii, vi, 189

National Parks Service, Museum Management Program and Fredrick Douglass National Historic Site, FRDO 3863, letter. http://www.nps.gov/history/museum/treasures/html/D/FRD03863.htm: page 90

Noble, Edward M. *History of Caroline County, Maryland from Its Beginning*. (Federalsburg, MD: J. W. Stowell, 1920): page 9

New York Public Library, Photographs and Prints Division, Schomburg Center for Research in Black Culture, Astor, Lenox and Tilden Foundations: pages 3, 4, 23, 34, 36, 50, 52, 74, 86, 94, 117

New York Public Library, Eno Collection, Miriam and Ira Wallach Division of Art, Prints and Photographs, The New York Public Library, Astor Lennox and Tilden Foundations: page 58

Rochester Images: From the Collection of the Rochester Public Library Local History Division (e.g. rpf 02425 and rpf02343): page 72

Stowe, Harriet Beecher. Stern, Philip Van Doren, ed. *The Annotated Uncle Tom's Cabin*. (New York: Paul S. Ericksson, Inc, 1964): pages 14, 29

INDEX

JM

```
--         Adler, David A.
B
Douglass Frederick Douglass.
A
```

$18.95

DATE			

BAKER & TAYLOR